The Hong Kong Economic Policy Studies Series

INSTITUTIONAL DEVELOPMENT OF THE INSURANCE INDUSTRY

INSTITUTIONAL DEVELOPMENT OF THE INSURANCE INDUSTRY

Ben T. Yu

Published for
The Hong Kong Centre for Economic Research
The Hong Kong Economic Policy Studies Forum
by

City University of Hong Kong Press

First published 1997
Printed in Hong Kong

ISBN 962-937-007-7

Published by
City University of Hong Kong Press
City University of Hong Kong
Tat Chee Avenue, Kowloon, Hong Kong

Internet: http://www.cityu.edu.hk/upress/
E-mail: upress@cityu.edu.hk

The free-style calligraphy on the cover, *bao*, means "*to insure*" in Chinese.

Contents

Detailed Chapter Contents

Foreword

The key to the economic success of Hong Kong has been a business and policy environment which is simple, predictable and transparent. Experience shows that prosperity results from policies that protect private property rights, maintain open and competitive markets, and limit the role of the government.

The rapid structural change of Hong Kong's economy in recent years has generated considerable debate over the proper role of economic policy in the future. The impending restoration of sovereignty over Hong Kong from Britain to China has further complicated the debate. Anxiety persists as to whether the pre-1997 business and policy environment of Hong Kong will continue.

During this period of economic and political transition in Hong Kong, various interested parties will be re-assessing Hong Kong's existing economic policies. Inevitably, some will advocate an agenda aimed at altering the present policy making framework to reshape the future course of public policy.

For this reason, it is of paramount importance for those familiar with economic affairs to reiterate the reasons behind the success of the economic system in the past, to identify what the challenges are for the future, to analyze and understand the economy sector by sector, and to develop appropriate policy solutions to achieve continued prosperity.

In a conversation with my colleague Y. F. Luk, we came upon the idea of inviting economists from universities in Hong Kong to take up the challenge of examining systematically the economic policy issues of Hong Kong. An expanding group of economists (The Hong Kong Economic Policy Studies Forum) met several times to give form and shape to our initial ideas. The Hong Kong Economic Policy Studies Project was then launched in 1996 with some 30 economists from the universities in Hong Kong and a few from overseas. This is the first time in Hong Kong history that a concerted public effort has been undertaken by academic economists in the territory. It represents a joint expression of our collective concerns, our hopes for a better Hong Kong, and our faith in the economic future.

The Hong Kong Centre for Economic Research is privileged to be co-ordinating this Project. The unfailing support of many distinguished citizens in our endeavour and their words of encouragement are especially gratifying. We also thank the directors and editors of the City University of Hong Kong Press and The Commercial Press (H.K.) Ltd. for their enthusiasm and dedication which extends far beyond the call of duty.

Yue-Chim Richard Wong
Director
The Hong Kong Centre
for Economic Research

Foreword by Series Editor

The insurance industry has been a significant part of Hong Kong's financial sector, and local insurance business is expanding fast. At present, the industry is facing at least two broad categories of issues.

First, as a result of financial deregulation and innovation in developed economies, the lines dividing traditional financial activities have become blurred. Given Hong Kong's economic and financial openness and rising number of foreign financial institutions, the insurance industry must re-position itself to take advantage of changing environments.

Second, economic reform and fast growth in Mainland China have generated enormous demand for insurance services there. Despite the very restrictive official barriers to enter China's yet-to-be developed but huge market, it is still sufficiently attractive to capture the close attention of Hong Kong insurance companies, the more so now when the two economies are getting ever closer.

These two external factors, together with rapid development of the industry itself, warrant a detailed examination of the current situation and regulatory framework of Hong Kong's insurance industry. Moreover, to the extent that insurance companies are financial intermediaries and institutional investors, changes in the industry do affect the savings pattern and the channelling of funds in the economy, and may thus have macroeconomic implications.

The literature on the economic analysis of insurance is vast, but it is mostly theoretical and not directly applicable to the case of Hong Kong. On the other hand, in Hong Kong existing publications on insurance focus mainly on technical practices of the profession. This book fills the gap by discussing insurance in Hong Kong within a framework of economic analysis.

The author, Dr. Ben T. Yu, first discusses insurance in general, highlighting the insights of the theory of transaction costs. He then goes on to review the development of the insurance industry in Hong Kong, addresses the above issues in detail, and comes up with some policy recommendations. Professionals in insurance and finance, as well as policy-makers will all find this book a useful reference.

Y. F. Luk
School of Economics and Finance
The University of Hong Kong

Foreword by Professor F. L. Leung

It has not been easy for Dr. Yu to study the insurance industry of Hong Kong because commercial firms guard their business policies and data from researchers, and because the literature written about the insurance industry is only a poor shadow to that about banks. Indeed, Dr. Yu deserves extra credit for embarking upon this bold, policy-oriented project. This treatise goes beyond what its title suggests. Projecting China's enormous insurance market, Dr. Yu recommends attemptable strategies such as forming strategic alliances with the lesser-known regional insurance corporations and banks in China. He also lays plain ways to develop, train, and upgrade the standard and image of insurance professionals in Hong Kong. Professionals in China and the Pacific basin will benefit from such strategies and educational development in the medium and long run.

Regarding insurance, reinsurance, Mandatory Provident Fund and captives, Dr. Yu takes pains to describe how Hong Kong can exploit its competitive advantages, and how Hong Kong suffers from institutional disadvantages vis-a-vis well-developed centers such as Bermuda and U.S. Virgin Islands. Hong Kong claims to be a developed financial center of world-class. Yet, its insurance industry until recent times has been neglected by the policy-makers in the government. Although many legislations have been enacted, more remains to be done. Dr. Yu proposed some legislative reforms.

Hong Kong will have much to offer in terms of experiences and knowledge to serve China and East Asia in providing insurance services. This book provides a brief academic introduction to that scenario. Government policy-makers, insurance professionals and lawyers in and out of Asia should find Dr. Yu's findings worthy of serious reading and pondering.

Frankie Fook-lun Leung
Adjunct Professor of Law
Loyola Law School, Los Angeles;
Lecturer, School of Law
Stanford University, Palo Alto.
March 1997

Preface

The project cannot be completed within a short time period without the help of many people. I have benefited greatly form contacts introduced by friends, and friends of the friends in the industry. The list is too long to be listed here, but I want to say emphatically that without their generous comments and assistance, the project will be impossible to be conducted. My official source of information are from the Census and Statistics Department, the Insurance Authority, and the Vocational Training Council of the Hong Kong Government, the Hong Kong Bank and several past studies of the Hong Kong insurance industries. The position adopted in this study, however, does not reflect any of the institutional positions listed above.

Research expense on this project has come from the Hong Kong Centre of Economic Research, the School of Economics and Finance at the University of Hong Kong, and a supplementary year-end grant from the University of Hong Kong. I wish to thank the Social Science Research Center of the University of Hong Kong for conducting the telephone survey, and my research assistants Michael Cheung and Pamela Lam for their conscientious and diligent works.

Ben T. Yu
School of Economics and Finance
The University of Hong Kong

List of Illustrations

Figures

Tables

Institutional Development of the Insurance Industry

CHAPTER 1

Introduction

All over the Asia-Pacific region, deregulation and the increasingly sophisticated to keep pace with technology have enabled insurers and reinsurers to transform their industry an economic miracle sweeping across their region. In Hong Kong, insurance reform is taking an interesting twist, and possibly a U-turn. Hong Kong has a background slightly different from those of the other Asia-Pacific economies in that Hong Kong's industry has never been heavily regulated. In fact, considering the long history of Hong Kong's insurance industry, which can be traced back to as early as 1841, it is rather amazing that the first comprehensive ordinance governing the operation of the insurance companies was not put into effect until 1983. For 142 years prior to that, insurance in Hong Kong has operated primarily as a laissez faire industry.

During the twelve-year period between 1983 and 1995 there have been twenty-eight amendment ordinances and pieces of subsidiary legislation enacted.[1] Such changes have occurred most rapidly over the last two years, with five amendment ordinances and pieces of subsidiary legislation being introduced in 1994 and eight being introduced in 1995 — almost half the total number of amendment ordinances and pieces of subsidiary legislation introduced since 1983. Indeed, the current atmosphere in the insurance industry in Hong Kong is not so much one of deregulation as one in which the central question is of how to regulate. The term *atmosphere* is used here to represent something that has not yet taken its final shape, but that reflects an ongoing dialogue within the evolving industry and between the government and the industry. Despite the large number of new acts that have been introduced, there are questions as to whether or not any piece of legislation is truly binding. There is also room for discussions of whether constraints are self regulated or government imposed. The industry at this stage is too young to evaluate the new acts but too old to support an argument for the maintenance of the status quo.

This study is about the future direction of the industry, and about what changes, if any, need to be made. We must first recognize the fact that industry should not be regulated purely for the sake of regulation. Regulations are set up in response to problems and issues raised by an industry. Some problems are isolated incidents and can only be dealt with on an ad hoc basis, while others reflect a growing structural and institutional trend. Institutional problems cannot be easily identified and they must be studied by using a combination of theories and observations. Only after having completed a broad review of the industry might one perhaps be able to identify a structural or an institutional trend. These are the basic question this study is asking. From what angle are we going to evaluate the industry? What precautions and actions can be suggested by looking at the industry from such an angle? What are the industry's practical problems, and how ought we to analyze them?

A Restatement of the Paradigm of Debate

At this junction of economic and policy transition in Hong Kong, the insurance industry and the government will have to confront many specific policies. It may be useful to go back to the fundamental paradigm of debate that the Registrar General of the Hong Kong Government posted in his speech to the industry 15 years ago, just before the first comprehensive Insurance Ordinance of Hong Kong was installed. Speaking at an annual dinner for the industry in 1981,[2] Mr. Piers Jacobs referred in the following way to a 1971 UNCTAD report based on an "Expert Group on Insurance Legislation and Supervision":

> "The experts also pointed out repeatedly that insurance supervision, while playing the traditional role for which it has been originally established, namely the protection of policy-holders, beneficiaries and their parties, should also take constantly into account the general economic, social and other national interests."

To this opinion, Mr. Jacobs countered,

> "I very much doubt whether we in Hong Kong will have any inclination to extend Government intervention to this extent. We are concerned with the stability of insurance companies for the purposes of protecting policyholders. The contribution made by the insurance industry to the economy is something that will be regulated by the operation of the free market system. It is for the market place to decide what contribution is to be made to the economy by any particular industry. In general terms only if the activities of an industry were to place the economy in jeopardy would there be a case for Government intervention in this area. We do not see the task of insurance supervision as being a tool of economic policy, and in this we perhaps differ from many Insurance Commissioners in the region."

Realistically, Hong Kong has already departed to some extent from the spirit behind the first comprehensive Insurance Ordinance of 1983. While the future direction of the industry may still be uncertain, it is difficult to imagine that the industry will revert altogether to its original pre-1983 position, as articulated by Mr. Jacobs. The industry is asking new questions now. These questions need to be evaluated on their own merit. But at the highest level of policy making, one cannot escape the fundamental philosophical debate as posted by Mr. Jacobs. If the spirit behind the 1983 Ordinance is to be maintained, proposed changes may have to be kept at a minimum, leaving the market to weed out losers. On the other hand, if a new direction for the industry is to be pursued, a study of the underlying trends and the economic environment affecting the industry may help design the institutional structure needed for the implementation of this new direction. Such a study is what we are attempting here. If the choice is between doing something and doing nothing, it may be best to do nothing. But if one is determined to do something and is trying to decide which direction to take, one must draw on theory and evidence in order to choose wisely and to minimize mistakes.

Methodology

We propose to study the practical problems of Hong Kong's insurance industry from a theoretical perspective as well as from an industry perspective. The former is an academic approach that articulates a concept (or a model) and tests the deduced hypotheses, while the latter approach focuses on issues raised within the industry and searches for a theory that can give answers to these issues. The former goes from theory to facts, the latter from facts to theory. The two approaches overlap somewhat, but they do not always coincide. This study uses more of the latter (inductive) approach. However, to the extent that a theoretical counterpart to practical issues can be found, some explanation of theories on insurance contracts, marketing, administration (service), investment, and financial strength will be reviewed in this book in order to set the stage for subsequent discussions. The theories discussed also include external factors of regulation and political developments, which will be examined in conjunction with issues dealing with Hong Kong's insurance industry.

This is not a purely academic study, so no attempts will be made to test hypotheses.[3] Indeed, data available for this study is too limited to allow for the performance of a rigorous statistical analysis in the academic sense of the term. However, that does not mean that theories are useless as a basis for discussion. For one thing, theories introduce a set of terminology that links the common elements in seemingly unrelated sets of observation. In this sense, this study approaches the question of insurance slightly differently than do studies more familiar to the practitioners. Studies of the insurance industry typically go through each sector of the industry one by one, starting with a type of general insurance and then going on to discuss various types of life products. Each type of insurance can occupy a separate chapter of such studies. The approach undertaken in this book will be different. We will start by offering an explanation of some general theories on contracting, marketing, and industrial organizations that could be useful for an understanding of the insurance field. We will then move on to discuss some practical issues of the Hong Kong insurance industry.

This study uses theory in two ways. First, it is used as a framework for identifying the problems of the insurance industry; the object is to look for real-world features of the industry that reveal the general principle. According to this methodology of a theory, the search should be confined to those aspects of the insurance business in Hong Kong that are encompassed by the theory. Second, this book uses theory not to identify problems as such, but for the purpose of helping to create a vocabulary; the object is to start a dialogue to shape a vision for the future. An example of the second use is various methods of articulating transaction costs and control rights of an industry. These academic concepts are not normally part of the vocabulary of the industry. However, drawing the industry's attention to such theoretical concepts may suggest new methods of articulating issues, and may thus point to new directions for improvement.

The institutional structure of the insurance industry in Hong Kong is presently going through some dynamic evolutionary changes. Demographics and technology innovations are dramatically altering the once-simple world of commerce. Although the changes are in a great part likely to be driven by these factors and by the investment needs of the community, many changes occur as a result of regulations from within and outside the industry. As broader integration between the economies of Hong Kong and China is expected to take place, the Hong Kong economy will have to confront changes. Hong Kong is not a transitional economy, but it has to deal with the problems of a transitional economy problems; such deal not only with individual choice of actions, but the collective choice of constraints.[4] We use theories in a transitional economy to explain the past and to provide guidelines for the future. In this sense, this study can only serve as a reference for policy makers. It cannot replace the work to be decided by the policy makers. After consulting this study, policy makers will have to make subjective judgments. Based on analyses this book, they should find it easier, though, to confront with regulatory problems about the insurance industry in the environment of the post-1997 era.

Categorization of the Main Issues to be Studied

The study will begin in Chapter 2 with theories taken from the industrial organization of insurance, with an emphasis on problems confronting transitional economies. At the fundamental level of infrastructure building, there is a need to establish some degree of conceptual understanding of the insurance marketplaces. We shall attempt to gain an understanding of the "moral hazard and adverse selection"; such are barriers to the operation of an efficient insurance market. These barriers have often been used to justify some sort of government intervention.

For transitional economies, reasons for intermittent intervention are particularly compelling; a basic understanding of how the market operates is therefore essential to prevent over-regulation. In the case of Hong Kong, transaction cost problems have been well understood in the past — relying mostly on private mechanisms to mitigate the transaction cost problems. The use of deductibles, coinsurance, and insurance limits have been explained in standard economic literature as methods of coping with these problems. In Hong Kong, industry practitioners and policy makers understand these mechanisms well, even in the absence of a formal theory. Nevertheless, this set of theory can still be stated as a point of reference regarding the future development of insurance contracts.

There are theoretical concepts other than those of moral hazard and adverse selection that affect the organization of an insurance industry. Some of these concepts can be mentioned as practical guidelines, others as a conceptualization of an industry practice. We will discuss the specific issue of "hold-ups" often discussed in the economic literature of contracting. Although the practice of hold-ups is probably a common one among practitioners, institutional measures to cope with this problem have not yet been developed in Hong Kong.

In the same vein is the theoretical question of the commission rate of insurance agents and of their relationships with companies. The interdependence of commission rates and premium rates set by insurance companies under competition is not an issue that is well understood by analysts outside the industry. Thus for this kind of inquiry, we hope to go from practice to theory. In the same chapter, we also look into reinsurance business and captives business. In order to determine what type of policies these two categories of business need, we must understand first what they are, and be familiar with the underlying economics leading to their formation.

The temporal flow of this book goes like this. It will first give an overview of Hong Kong's insurance industry. Chapter 3 is largely descriptive and historical. An Office of the Commissioner of Insurance was not established in Hong Kong until 1990. It came about after a restructuring of the Insurance Division of the Registrar General's Department took place in the same year. Prior to that, industry statistics were not collected by the Commissioner but by the Hong Kong's Census and Statistics Department whose data can still be used today to provide a different angle of observation for comparison.

In terms of the future direction of the industry, our discussion will be divided into three categories which are treated in Chapter 4 to Chapter 6. The first category has to do with the general guidelines of regulation. The overall problem concerning regulation is one of a balance between a hands-off approach and an upgraded standard of professionalism for the industry. Insurers' voluntary protection of their own reputations has thus far acted as the main source of protection for the insured. Up to this point in time, official regulation has been used minimally to back up professional action. Nevertheless, a new regulatory framework and regulatory issues are bound to surface in the future, with a dominant voice emanating from consumer groups (or from agents representing consumers). Regulation by government can be viewed as a political move to redistribute risk between the insurer and the insured. Hong Kong's future political economy is likely to lean towards this aspect of the regulation. In the extreme, one cannot rule out the possibility that consumer protection agencies will lobby governments with the object of minimizing risk to the insured by means of regulatory measures that may inhibit entry into the insurance business. The wisdom of allowing the insurance regulatory authority to operate completely independently of the operations of other financial branches will be discussed along with several specific regulatory issues.

The second category of practical issues to be addressed involves the development of a competitive edge for the insurance industry in Hong Kong. This is treated in Chapter 5. Competitive edge is a topical issue, especially now because Hong Kong wishes to maintain its financial position in Asia after 1997. The laissez faire approach to this issue would dictate that nothing be done, as though the invisible hand would automatically put Hong Kong where it should be in the Asian economy. Nevertheless if one is willing to assume, for the sake of argument, that some guidelines can sometimes be better than no guidelines, several suggestions (not prescriptions) can be made. We shall argue that Hong Kong's special advantage is institutional development in terms of strategic alliances and the ability to put deals together. Encouraging efficient design of institutional arrangements across different industries and different areas may best utilize this advantage. The possibility of a strategic alliance with the Mainland China market, the possibilities of developing reinsurance and captives business in Hong Kong, and the emerging Mandatory Provident Fund factor will be discussed in later chapters.

The third and last category in which we will identify the future direction of insurance in Hong Kong has to do with improving public perception of the industry. We discuss this in Chapter 6 for the reason that we need to know how the public presently views the insurance industry. Comments on this topic have thus far been directed only towards life insurance, because public perception is known to be most important for this sector of the industry.

There are reasons to believe that the life insurance sector of the insurance industry occupies a unique place in the insurance business. To many families in Hong Kong, life insurance is not only insurance; it has a saving component as well. Life insurance issues are thus not purely insurance issues. They have to be considered in conjunction with other investment decisions. The issue of trust is more relevant in the life insurance business than in other areas of insurance. In the case of non-life insurance, e.g. insurance of property, liability and health, consumer at least has an opportunity of learning because periodic re-contracting is common. In the case of life insurance (as in the case of life insurance combined with pensions), contracts cover long periods of time are difficult to rescind without incurring heavy penalties. Acquiring the knowledge necessary to interpret contracts is very costly to the insured, who must rely on the reputation of the insurer. For these reasons, the attitude of the public towards life insurance as a product, the company as a provider of the product, and agents in terms of their knowledge of personal finance, may affect the way in which private and public policies are going to be formulated in the future. These issues will be summed up in the concluding chapter of this study, including with our suggestions and recommendations.

Notes

1. *Annual Report 1995*, Office of the Commissioner of Insurance and the Registrar of Occupational Retirement Schemes, Hong Kong.
2. *IIHK Journal*, The Insurance Institute of Hong Kong, July 1981.
3. This is Milton Friedman's methodology of positive economics.
4. See the methodology of James M. Buchanan, "The Domain of Constitutional Economics, "*Constitutional Political Economy*, Vol.1, No.1, 1990.

CHAPTER 2

The Industrial Organization of Insurance

Insurance is an important aspect of risk management. The basic premise underlying the need for insurance is self evident: individuals and firms are risk averse, they seek mechanisms by which to transfer all or part of their risk to others who might be more equipped to bear it. Individuals or companies likely to bear risk are those which are less risk averse, those which can pool different types of risks, and those which can offer insurance contracts simultaneously to a large number of buyers, thereby utilizing the advantage of the law of large numbers.[1]

There has been extensive economic treatment of the above notion of insurance. Aside from some early works,[2] well-recognized mathematical frameworks have been developed to back up basic intuition. These frameworks have (1) explained the role of different institutional arrangements for risk shifting including insurance markets, stock markets, futures markets, and sharing contracts of various types in the economy, and (2) identified the theoretical conditions for optimal risk-pooling arrangements, showing that risk aversion can generally affect the optimal coverage (i.e., optimal shares) of people participating in the pool.[3]

Arrangements such as coinsurance and reinsurance can thus be derived on the basis of different degrees of risk aversion. The literature has therefore established a strong theoretical foundation for the existence of insurance.

A simple example will serve to illustrate the way in which one's degree of risk aversion is related to insurance. Suppose a woman is willing to pay $50 to avoid losing her cat, which is valued at $200. The woman is said to be risk averse if, based on a probability calculation with an estimated probability of loss of 25%, the expected value of loss is less than $50. A man who collects statistics on lost cats may know the probability of loss to be only 10%. If the man can offer an insurance contract to many cat lovers at a premium of slightly more than $20, the law of large numbers implies that he will make money in the long run with perfect certainty. The contract will leave both the woman and the man gaining from the transaction. The woman is willing to pay $50 to avoid risk, and she winds up paying only slightly more than $20. The man makes a small "profit," in the amount above $20 that he receives.

A slight modification of the example also suggests the reason why the law of large numbers and the man's ability to perfectly diversify risk is not necessary for the insurance contract. Suppose the man knows only one cat lover, this woman, but he owns a cat farm. A loss of a cat to the man may mean very little, and he will gladly offer an insurance contract to replace the woman's cat in the event of its loss. Even if the man does not own a cat farm, as long as his willingness to pay for the loss of a cat is less than $50 (let's say $40) an insurance contract can be written at a premium of somewhere between $50 and $40 so that both parties will be better off. Of course, the man in this case will need at least one cat, hopefully, one that is identical to that of the woman's.

Data Collection and Statistical Estimation

The economic foundation of insurance mentioned above, is, unfortunately, not very useful when it comes to generating implications regarding the way in which insurance contracts can be drafted or how the insurance industry is organized. After all, the insurance industry existed long before economists formalized its existence. The first life insurance company in the United States (the Presbyterian Ministers' Fund in Philadelphia) was established in 1759 and is still in existence. Lloyd's of London set up shop in 1688 in a London coffee house owned by Edward Lloyd. Even Adam Smith, the founding father of classical economics, wrote about the insurance industry in his 1776 *Wealth of Nations*. The current implications for industries in transitional economies may be quite different from those suggested by the theorists of economic models of insurance, which emphasize risk-aversion. It is perhaps in the use of statistical principles and in the implied need to gather statistical data in the setting of an efficient premium for insurance that the theoretical models have provided insights for the industry.

Today, statistical techniques are not just research tools; they are a means for gaining a competitive edge in the insurance industry. Under competition, insurance companies that have better information than do other insurance companies about the probability of loss can set a premium that more accurately reflects their costs and can thus survive longer in business. The more accurately an insurance company can estimate the loss probability of the insured, the higher will be the anticipated profit, which will be translated into a larger market share in the long run. This issue is particularly relevant for transitional economies, as the mechanisms for the setting of premiums are absent. The type of products likely to have a market may, in addition to depending on the socioeconomic and cultural constraints the society is facing, also depend on the estimation of accident rates. Being in possession of these statistics may contribute to the rapid development of these markets. Indeed, it can be argued that the role of actuaries, who are professionals in charge of setting and evaluating accident rates and premiums, may expand in these emerging markets. It is because data collection could become just as important as statistical interpretation of the data.

Determining the sequential steps necessary to develop insurance industries in transitional economies is always challenging for economic reformers. It is easy to say that once a market is open the forces of competition will automatically produce efficient results, but sometimes reality does not immediately cooperate. The reason is that foreign insurers can have as much if not more difficulty collecting data in transitional economies. Practical concerns such as the setting of premiums, the appropriate level of reserves, and the introduction of new products cannot be easily transferred from the home country of a foreign insurer. In short, the collection of statistical information and the development of indigenous practitioners has to go hand-in-hand with the opening up of the market.

Contractual Considerations

Perhaps more important than the issue of risk estimation and the optimal sharing of risk are issues dealing with the contractual relationship between buyer and seller. In the absence of statistical calculations, the setting of premium is market driven. Conceptually, an insurance contract can be written between a buyer and a seller for just about anything, subject to the problems of adverse selection and moral hazard (to be described). Such a contract can be for a small item like a portable radio, or for a large project like the launching of satellites. The more familiar types of insurance are motor insurance, property insurance, health insurance, and life insurance. Less familiar types involve the insurance of obscure events, such as insurance on the award of one million pounds for the capture of the monster assumed to live in Loch Ness, Scotland.[4]

Every day we face the possible occurrence of unexpected or catastrophic events that could lead to financial losses. Insurance against these events is normally classified into one of two types: life insurance and property and casualty insurance (general insurance). The former is sold by life insurance companies that provide income if the policyholder dies, retires, or is incapacitated by illness. The latter is sold by general insurance companies that specialize in policies that pay for losses incurred as a result of accidents, fire, or theft. Those companies that sell both types of insurance policies are often called composite insurance companies.

The subject of insurance does not cover only private catastrophic events. Social phenomena such as unemployment and bank deposits have often been included as part of the discussion of insurance, in the form, for example, of unemployment insurance for the labour force of a country, and bank deposit insurance to protect the general public's money against the risk of banks going bankrupt.[5] These programmes have often been viewed as the exclusive territory of government administration. However, a choice actually exists between private versus public insurance. The contractual approach can be used as an appropriate conceptual framework in this context. The relevant question is whether, under competition, government insurance contracts are more or less efficient than private insurance. The focus of this question differs depending on the specific context in which it is asked. In the U.S. health sector, for example, the question may be how to go from private to public insurance, but in China's health sector, the question may be how to go from public to private. In addition, the subject of insurance also includes the choice between public and self insurance. Family as the most primitive form of insurance has been well recognized.[6] Places like Hong Kong have traditionally adopted a self-insurance approach to various types of risk management problems such as retirement savings, unemployment, and bank deposit insurance.

Whether one focuses on government insurance or private insurance, social insurance or self insurance, the contractual approach addresses three important problems in the transfer of risk. These problems are adverse selection, moral hazard, and specific holdups.[7] The origin of these three sets of problems is asymmetric information, that is, information known to one but not to both contracting parties. Asymmetric information opens up the possibility of cheating and misrepresentation and has led to a large volume of theoretical literature on what has been called the principal-agent problem.[8]

The literature on principal-agent issues is too lengthy to cite and summarize here.[9] Given positive transaction costs in the real world, adverse selection and moral hazard problems have often been manifested to different degrees in different types of insurance. In situations in which the problems are not very severe, certain signalling and monitoring mechanisms exist either as a precondition or as part of a contractual provision in the risk transfer contract. While it is better not to have such problems than to have them, the existence of moral hazard and adverse selection will not necessarily eradicate the market. Only when the moral hazard and adverse selection problems are very severe does risk becomes uninsurable, in which case a market for a particular type of insurance will not exist. In these instances, there will be no insurance contracts even if there is a demand for risk reduction and even if someone wishes to offer insurance.[10]

Adverse Selection

Asymmetric information in adverse selection occurs before the transaction takes place.[11] For example, the people who need health insurance the most are likely to be the unhealthy ones. Only buyers who think a given premium is favourable will purchase insurance. Thus, the customer base of an insurance contract that is uniformly available to everyone will adversely select out the bad risk. As an example, a person suffering from a terminal disease would want to take out the biggest life and medical insurance policies possible. Similarly, the type of insurance companies that offer ridiculously low premiums are likely to be bad-risk companies. It might be the case that they are either desperate for funding or have no intention of honouring their obligations. If either of the above-mentioned problems is severe, no one will want to offer insurance contracts to any buyers, and no buyers will trust any insurance providers. In order words, an insurance market cannot exist in this situation.[12]

Adverse selection problems in insurance can often be mitigated by various types of "signals," or by what is called brand-name advertising. Thus, an insurance company with a long history obviously has a better reputation than a start-up company; and the established company can inspire more confidence in its customers. In theory, at least, a company must operate for a sufficient length of time in order to reap the return from its advertising and early investment. Companies that demonstrate a bigger commitment are less likely to cheat on their customers.

Many countries do recognize the problem of adverse selection in their supervision of the insurance industry. For example, in

China, foreign companies have to maintain representative offices for a long time before finally being granted licenses. Of course, there is a limit to the effectiveness of such requirements; an overly demanding initial commitment can evolve as a form of protectionism and would hurt rather than benefit the industry. In contrast, Hong Kong's licensing requirements are not severe by international standards. That does not mean that Hong Kong lacks the mechanism to counter adverse selection. New entrants still pay heavily in terms of other forms of commitment such as advertising, a higher commission, better office location, and so on. Indeed, the low failing rate of insurance companies in Hong Kong has suggested that these private remedies for adverse selection may be quite effective.

Remedies to counter the effects of adverse selection also exist in the form of insurance companies' screening of potential buyers. The screening can be done on the basis of signals acquired by the buyer or on the basis of insurance companies' pricing strategies. Signals acquired by the buyer are things like his or her driving record, the type of car that is insured, and the age and marital status of the individual. Life insurance salespeople typically ask potential clients questions about their smoking habits, drug and alcohol use, and other behaviours that could potentially affect their health. Objective medical evaluations using blood and urine samples are also common procedures through which bad risks can be selected out. Screening on the basis of pricing strategies implies that the insurance market is segmented, with different insurance companies serving different types of customers.[13] In any case, an effective compilation procedure for information is an important management principle of insurance.

Moral Hazard

Moral hazard is a situation in which party A and party B are bound by a contract, and party B's behaviour (which cannot be observed by party A) violates the intent of the contract to the detriment of party A, or vice versa. The nature of asymmetric information in moral hazard occurs after the transaction.[14] Usually, it refers to a unilateral, one-sided, unobservable action taken by one party to a transaction. Such an action reduces the expected benefits to the other party. A person might be perfectly healthy at the time he or she enters into a health insurance contract with an insurance company. However, because the person knows that he or she is insured, he or she has less of an incentive to take care of his or her own health after the insurance contract is signed. Using the terminology of a principal-agent problem, moral hazard results from the costly monitoring of the efforts of the agents. Presumably, policyholders can agree to exercise due care on the property (including their own lives) under insurance, but it is costly for the insurance company to check on the policyholders' promise. If premiums have to be raised to an exorbitant level to cover recklessness or, in the extreme, deliberate abuse of the insured property, individuals would choose to self insure rather than pay the price of an insurance policy. Once again, if the problem becomes severe enough, it may cause the market to disappear.

Like adverse selection, problems of moral hazard can occur with buyers as easily as they do with sellers; that is, they can occur with the insurer as easily as they do with the insured. For example, relying on a steady incoming premium income, an insurer might invest in "excessively" risky assets, thus jeopardizing the reliability of the insurance funds from which claims would have to be drawn. Any post-contractual services of the insurer, such as the processing of claims, responses to inquiries, granting of new loans, or even the insurer's internal policy insofar as the agent's turnover rates are affected, can all in one form or another contribute to the moral hazard problem on the part of the insurer. This problem and that of the insured are completely symmetrical. If policyholders do not have confidence in the operation of the insurance company, this lack of trust may, again, eradicate the market.

Remedies for the moral hazard problem can be implemented in several ways. Restrictive provisions are often included in an insurance contract to indirectly monitor difficult-to-observe behaviour. For example, health insurance providers cannot monitor the eating and drinking patterns of policyholders on a daily basis, but a contract can require that the insured receive a regular physical check-up as a condition for the issuance and the continuation of the insurance. Companies offering rental motor bike insurance may not be able to monitor the behaviour of the user directly, but the requirement that helmets be worn as a condition for renting the bike can to some extent reduce the probability of loss. Contractual provisions such as deductibles, coinsurance, and limiting the amount of insurance that can be purchased are some additional ways of reducing the moral hazard problems of insurance.[15]

The presence of deductibles, coinsurance, and insurance limits in various insurance contracts also reflect the spectrum of moral hazard problems. A deductible is the fixed amount that a loss has to exceed before a policy begins to pay. For small losses that do not exceed the deductible, the insured is fully responsible. Deductibles are necessary if moral hazard for small losses are severe. For example, if their auto insurance had no deductible, drivers would not be as careful when steering their cars into tight spaces in a carpark as they would be if their insurance had a deductible, because they know that if they scratch the paint on their fender the insurance company will pay to have it repaired. On the other hand, one does not expect the moral hazard of a complete car wreck to be severe, and therefore there is usually full insurance for major collisions.[16]

A related problem on the spectrum of moral hazard problem is over-insurance. An over-insured person may deliberately "lose" his or her property in order to make a claim whose value is higher than that of the property. Again, using automobile insurance as an example, if a person is allowed to insure his car for more than its worth, he is likely to leave the keys in the ignition when he leaves the car, because he can make money by doing so. This is also why Arrow (1963) said, "a fire insurance policy for more than the value of the premises might be an inducement to arson or at least to carelessness." The problem of over-insurance is particularly severe in the case of unique property, when the owner's assessment of an item's worth can often be higher than the item's market value. By allowing the limit to be set above the market value, insurance companies would have to conduct additional monitoring to prevent moral hazard from occurring. For example, they might demand that an elaborate alarm system be installed.[17]

There are instances of losses where the moral hazard problems apply evenly to every level of loss. For example, the moral hazard problem for the first pill a patient takes may be similar to the moral hazard problem for the nth pill the patient is going to take. In that case, the use of coinsurance, that is, the insured obtaining a fixed percentage of loss for reimbursement, could be arranged to reduce moral hazard for all levels of losses within this spectrum. A policyholder who suffers a loss along with the insurance company has less of an incentive to act "wastefully", for example, by going to the doctor unnecessarily.

Moral hazard can affect insurance companies, too, but they take a different approach to the problem. In addition to government enforcement provided through some type of insurance authority, the organizational structure of an insurance company itself can provide some enforcement mechanisms to deal with internal moral hazard problems. For example, if policyholders also own the firm, they have the right to monitor some of the company's performance characteristics. It is for this reason that insurance companies sometimes offer their policyholders a type of "profit sharing" scheme. One is unlikely to choose this type of scheme in the hope of earning an abnormally high return. If a policyholder wishes to maximize the return on his investment, he would choose investment-linked contracts instead. In this sense, a profit-participating insurance scheme may be viewed as a monitoring scheme rather than as a "profit-sharing" scheme in the sense in which one usually thinks of the term. The relationship of firms' organizational structure to the performance of insurance companies has been analysed in a series of articles in the literature.[18]

Specific Hold-ups

The idea of specific hold-ups refers not only to a unilateral change in the effort of a contracting party, as in the case of moral hazard, but to a change in the terms and conditions *after* the transaction has taken place.[19] In order for this to occur, there must be, in addition to the assumption of asymmetric information, a costly switch-over of existing contractual relationships. Thus, a contractual relationship can be "locked in," not by agreement but by the inertia of human relationships and by the high cost of switch-overs. The issue can be discussed in the context of an insurance company and its clients as well as in the context of an insurance company and its agents.

The most common form of alleged hold-ups of an insurance company to its clients occurs in claims settlement. The fine print of an insurance contract can be ambiguous and can be subjected to a wide range of interpretations when claims are made. Consumer advocates argue that customers do not themselves carefully study this fine print before signing a contract, and hiring an attorney for the signing of an insurance contract would certainly be too costly. Naturally, it is too late to switch to another insurance company once a claim needs to be made. Another form of a hold-up has to do with the renewal of an existing contract. A client may routinely purchase the same insurance from the same source when an existing contract expires. This opens up the possibility of the insurance company charging a higher rate to take advantage of the specific relationship.[20] Because of the existence of these possibilities, premium setting in many countries requires the prior approval of the commissioner. In Hong Kong, such prior approval is not required. Thus, for either form of hold-up, the ultimate balancing force is the brand name of the insurer.

Hold-up possibilities can also occur between an insurance company and its agents. The essence of such controversies has to do with the client list. The client list is the joint production of the insurance company and the agents. Industry people sometimes compare the relationship of the insurance company and the agents to the clients to the relationship of a marriage to a child. When an agent leaves a company, it is like the breakup of a marriage, which raises the question of who will have custody of the child. As it does in the settling of a marital dispute, the expenditure necessary to raise a child comes to bear on this issue. As Grossman and Hart (1963) put it,

> "An insurance company has a number of expenditures . . . that can create ex post surplus between the insurance company and its agents or brokers. These expenditures include training of agents, client list-building expenditures (such as advertising), product development, and policyholder services. An insurance agent can have similar expenditures. To the extent that the efforts of the parties in generating these expenditures are not verifiable, they cannot be reimbursed directly without the creation of moral hazards (p. 711)."

This idea is related to the concept of "control rights" that is discussed in one branch of economic literature. Marvel (1982) observes that in the U.S. the relative importance of the independent agency system varies according to the type of insurance and the extent of insurers' financed promotional expenses (21). For example, in the area of surety insurance, an independent agency system has a market share as high as 96.3%. The independent agency system is used more frequently than is direct writing in the business lines than in the personal lines. Indeed, when commercial automobile bodily injury liability was compared with private automobile bodily injury liability, the market shares of the independent agency were notably higher in the former than in the latter (88.8% as opposed to 47.4%). Grossman and Hart (1986) complement this observation by noting that whole life insurance (with saving components) has a relatively small market share in the channel of distribution through independent agents/brokers. The market share, however, is higher for term insurance (without saving components), which must be renewed every year (see Grossman and Hart 1986, p. 715).

The studies conducted by Marvel and by Grossman and Hart

could potentially raise some theoretical inquiries in an important area of Hong Kong's insurance industry. Namely, they could bring up the nature of "control rights" in the industry, or the contractual relationship between agents/brokers and the firm (the insurer) in the industry. In additional to the promotional and mass media advertising expenditure that Marvel points out, Grossman and Hart suggest that the issue is related to the ownership of the client list. They suggest hold-up possibilities in the sense that an insurance company might opportunistically change the terms of a contract at the time of contract renewal, thus hurting the client. Simultaneously, the agent might divert a customer to another insurance company after the agent's employer has expended advertising efforts, thereby hurting the original insurer. The argument raises the possibility that in the case of products for which insurance is not automatically renewed and which are sensitive to an agent's actions, the agent will be more likely to own the client list; in other words, to operate as an independent agent. Alternatively, in the case of products for which insurance renewal is more certain and is less sensitive to the agent's actions, the company will be more likely to own the client list; that is, to operate as direct writers. Grossman and Hart's conjecture is supported by the observation that "about 65% of the premiums in property-casualty (general) insurance are generated by agents who own the client list, while in life insurance about 12% of the premiums are generated by agents who own the list" (Grossman and Hart 1986, p. 714).

Commission Rates and Compensation Issues

The question of the limits or the boundaries of a firm (or the question of control rights) also has to do with how commission rates are charged. The general nature of the problem has been summarized in a large volume of literature on sharecropping and principal-agent problems. Early writings on the subject by Cheung (1969) and Ross (1973) capture the essence of the problem by dealing with the way in which the sharing ratio, or the commission rate between the insurance companies and their agents, is determined. Recent literature provides more sophisticated modifications of this early work without changing the substance of the approach to the problem. Intuitively, one could speculate that the role of agents in selling insurance probably varies greatly depending on the type of insurance and the insurance company. Economic theory on contracting suggests that risk considerations are not the only issue affecting the size of an agent's commission. When agents play a more significant role in underwriting an insurance contract, they will receive a larger commission.

Webb, Launie, Rokes, and Baglini (1984, pp. 58–60) point out that agents in the U.S. receive two kinds of commissions: (1) a straight or sliding-scale percentage commission, and (2) a contingent or profit-sharing commission. The former type of commission is paid at the inception of the policy, and it varies by type of insurance and by classification within a type. The latter is paid periodically — annually, semi-annually, or quarterly. It varies with the volume, rate of growth, and the loss ratio of the business an agent has placed with the insurer.

Not all insurance agents receive a commission based on premium. Agents working as employees of an insurer, e.g., those engaged in direct sales, usually receive a salary and little or no commission. Even brokers' compensation may not be entirely in the form of commissions. Some brokers charge fees for their services either in lieu of or in addition to commissions. Indeed, with today's brokers more and more often offering risk management services, the trend is moving towards service fees. In that case, the broker acts more or less as a consulting service.[21] Indeed, a recent International Risk Management fax survey found that out of a sample of 64 brokers, "about half the respondents pay their brokers on a fee basis — ranging from 37.5% of firms in Europe to 66% in the U.S., with an average of 50% worldwide. Comparatively, only 23% firms pay their brokers on a commission basis, with this method being favoured more in Europe than in the U.S. Annual retainers were the least favored method of payment — only 9% of firms used this method."[22]

Commission Rate Structure and Intertemporal Dynamics

A recent extension of the basic principal-agent problem to multiperiod interaction also considers the issue of backloading commission as described in Grossman and Hart (1986). Backloading commission refers to giving an insurance agent a larger commission for the renewal of a contract than for its initiation. In other words, the issue of commission can be studied not only in terms of a given level for a given line of business, but in terms of the structure of that rate with respect to the question of renewal, the age of a policy, etc. For life insurance, an insurer who wants to "take the money and run" is likely to offer an "abnormally" high commission rate for the first year. The objective is to get the business: if the insured chooses to renew the contract, the insurer has nothing to lose, because with proper screening when the insurance contract is underwritten, the risk of the insured's death is not likely to increase drastically. If the insured chooses to discontinue the contract after the first or the second year, it will be even better for the insurer, since the surrender cash value is usually close to zero for the first few years after which a life insurance contract goes into effect.

Indeed, a so-called cut-throat competitive tactic may be to offer very low premium rates with very high commission rates. As long as the size of the claims is smaller than what was expected, the insurer will be doing well and will remain in business. Indeed, so long as the market is growing, with the total amount of the premiums an insurer receives increasing more quickly than the total amount of the claims against him, this practice will not cause him to move into a grey area of shaky solvency margins, nor will it increase the possibility of insurers failing to honour their contracts. The situation, however, is expected to be more problematic once the market becomes more saturated.

Reinsurance and Captives

To understand reinsurance, one must recognize the contractual relationship between an insurer and a reinsurer is *an ordinary insurance contract with a deductible*. An insurer can act as the *front* of a reinsurer in generating businesses, but a great proportion of the premium generated may be ceded to a reinsurer. The retained amount, from the point of view of the reinsurer, is a deductible. Obviously, the reinsurer incurs less expenditure per unit of premium in insuring this portion of the business, as the front insurers have to incur a large portion of the advertising, marketing, and management expenses necessary to bring in the business in the first place. Moral hazard, adverse selection, and hold-up problems apply to the relationship between the insurer and the reinsurer, just as they do to the relationship between the insurer and the insured. In light of the high cost of certain information, a reinsurer may have to trust that the risk the insurer has taken up was a good risk in the first place.[23] The relationship between an insurer and a reinsurer is likely to be longer term than are the "retail-type" relationships that exist between insurers and the public.

Captives are related to reinsurers, but the two are not identical. Captives existed before World War II; the motivation behind its formation is multinational corporation wanting to self-insure.[24] A large corporation that owns plants and properties at different locations in different countries may want to come up with a way to manage its risk. Initially, captives were established by corporations that set aside reserves in an "insurance fund" to meet anticipated losses. With the advent of stricter taxation, the reserves ceased to be tax exempt, unless the insurance fund was incorporated as a separate company. A captive insurance company can therefore be viewed as a device created to avoid the "unreasonable" taxation of a corporation that has decided to self-insure.

Nevertheless, there are also transaction costs reasons for forming captives.[25] Some companies choose to self-insure rather than to use direct insurance through the markets. For example, it can be argued on transaction costs grounds that a shipping company would also want to operate a transport insurance service. Hospital and health equipment companies, because they are in a good position to control the moral hazard problem, might also be in a position to offer health insurance. Indeed, any valid reason for vertical integration is also a valid reason for forming a captive. In this respect, the issue of captives is not purely a tax issue. Strategic alliances between banks and insurance companies, and between insurance companies and other lines of business, can also be viewed from this angle. We shall discuss this in more detail in Chapter 5.

Summary

This chapter reviews the basic elements of risk transfer and applies them in the context of transitional economies in which institutional choice is a key variable of consideration. Although there are many varieties of insurance, a review of the basic theory and of the various contractual issues of insurance contracts can identify the similarities between all forms of insurance. The insurers' fundamental role is to bear risk. But because of various transaction costs problems in insurance, insurance business requires monitoring, screening, and designs of insurance contracts. Internal organization can be designed to curb adverse selection and moral hazard. Problems arising from specific hold-ups can lead to institutional specification of the relationship between insurance companies and their agents. Competitive commission rate determination further defines the scope of a firm. A relationship exists between the premium rate and the commission rate that an insurance company pays its agents. Insurance companies can compete by offering high commission rates coupled with low premium rates for the purpose of acquiring market shares.

The review here brings out several policy implications. Aside from the need for data collection and statistical interpretation for more accurate risk evaluation, insurers who are better able to cope with adverse selection, moral hazard, and specific hold-up problems for a particular type of insurance will acquire a competitive advantage in that area of insurance. This guiding principle applies not only to a private insurance company in search of its market niche, but to government-administered insurance programmes as well. After all, social unemployment insurance and deposits insurance are known to have negative consequences. Unemployment insurance has led to observable unemployment in Britain, and the deposit insurance was allegedly the main cause of the American banking crisis in the late 1980s. These phenomena are related to the moral hazard and adverse selection problems described in this chapter. Reforms of these systems therefore should concentrate not only on improving the administration of the system, but also on addressing the more fundamental question of what type of institution can best handle various contractual problems.

Insurance practitioners may find our discussion in this chapter to be overly theoretical because in daily practice, they must regularly deal with mundane issues of personnel management, marketing, advertising, and investment in credibility and company image in order for their business to succeed. Indeed, the skills a successful practitioner requires have nothing to do with performing the basic task of an insurer, that is, of being a risk bearer. However, the elements of transaction costs identified in this chapter explain in part why a practitioner's practical skills are equally important to a risk bearer. Indeed, it can be argued that the only true insurers in the real world are reinsurance companies. The way the insurance industry is organized will be difficult to explain in the absence of transaction costs. A discussion of transaction costs therefore is crucial to the understanding of how reinsurance is organized. The same can be said of the issue of captives.

Notes

1. Old insurance texts went as far as to say that risk is insurable only if one can apply the law of large numbers.
2. Notably von Neumann and Morgenstern (1947), Friedman and Savage (1948), Allais (1953), Arrow (1953).
3. See Arrow (1965), Borch (1960, 1961, 1962).
4. See A. Brown (1973) *Hazard Unlimited. The Story of Lloyd's of London*, London: Peter Davies Ltd.
5. In the U.S., social security, unemployment insurance and the bank deposit insurance (FDIC) are the three much-researched government-sponsored insurance programmes.
6. For an economic analysis of self insurance, see Ehrlich and Becker (1972).
7. The first two problems, adverse selection and moral hazard, are well recognized in the insurance field, as they are in the economic literature. Arrow (1963) and Spence and Zeckhauser (1971), captured the nature of the problem. The third problem, the specific hold-up problem, has only recently been addressed in the economic literature.
8. The term was coined by Ross (1973). Subsequent modeling exercises along these lines have been numerous. A good summary of the literature is provided in Dionne and Harrington (1990).
9. The mathematical formulation attains a level of eloquence similar to that of the literature on risk allocation cited earlier. Similar to the situation described earlier regarding risk allocation literature versus actual risk allocation, contracts existed long before economists formulated the existence of contracts.
10. Another condition of uninsurable risk is for the probability of loss plus the ratio of selling expense as a percentage of premium to be greater than one. In that case, the premium would have to be greater than the value of the item insured, making the item uninsurable.
11. See Akerloff (1970) for the formulation of this so-called "lemon problem".
12. It is easy to recognize the importance of positive transaction costs in arriving at this assertion. Without information cost, the seller can charge a premium exactly matching the risk category of a buyer. Likewise, a buyer would have full information on the type of company and its CEO. The latter manage the fund made up partly by the buyers' money.
13. Theoretical models on different pricing strategies of insurance companies can be found in Pauly (1974), Rothschild and Stiglitz (1976), and Stiglitz

(1977). Different types of equilibrium concepts can be studied in this context. See Crocker and Snow (1985).

14. Arrow (1963) provides a clear definition of the term.

15. The structure of asymmetric information can influence the way in which the moral hazard problem is modeled. In general, different solutions are provided for different assumptions. Dionne and Harrington (1990) reviewed the literature.

16. Deductibles cannot be viewed as existing exclusively for the purpose of solving the moral hazard problem. Like other contractual mechanisms, they can serve the dual purposes of solving adverse selection problems, as well. See Arrow (1974), Moffet (1977), and Schlesinger (1981).

17. See Pauly (1974).

18. Hansmann (1985) and Mayers and Smith (1981, 1986, 1987, 1988).

19. The idea of hold-ups is described in Klein, Crawford, and Alchian (1978) and in Williamson (1974). The application of hold-ups in the insurance industry is attempted in Grossman and Hart (1986).

20. The hold-up possibility should be distinguished from situations in which there is a need to increase premium due to a higher accident rate or due to the aging of a person, as in the case of term insurance (i.e. life insurance without savings). However, because the person may not have information about the changing accident rates and the increase in death probability as he ages, he may not know whether the increase in premium is excessive or not.

21. See Valerie Denney, "US Brokers: Times Are Changing". The Winchester Group, *Global Risk Manager 1996*. Another writer, Arthur Piper in *The Review: Worldwide Reinsurance* also commented, "Clients want added value advice based on balance sheet realities rather than off the shelf products".

22. "How Much Do You Pay Your Broker?" by Navin Reddy, 1995.

23. The theoretical foundation of reinsurance can be found in Borch (1962). The intention of our discussion here is to interpret reinsurance from a transaction costs perspective. The approach is more akin to the industry approach, as, for example, that found in Ho (1995), section 4.

24. Borch (1989), p. 273.

25. Indeed, as is pointed out in Bawcutt (1991), captives existed even in the absence of taxation worries.

CHAPTER 3

The Insurance Industry of Hong Kong

Insurance is a nontrivial division of Hong Kong's financial sector which consists of insurance and other finance services. Table 3.1 provides quantitative measures of the importance of the insurance industry relative to other finance services. The Hong Kong government, in its annual estimation of gross domestic product (GDP), defines "finance services" to include financial intermediation services such as banks, deposit-taking companies, firms dealing with personal loans, mortgages, instalment credit, and factoring and bill discounting. Also included in this category are investment and holding companies and brokers or dealers in stocks, futures, foreign exchange and gold bullion.[1] The government's definition of "insurance services" is relatively simple. It includes life and general insurers, insurance agents, and specialist firms providing professional insurance services. The two divisions' relative importance can be ranked in terms of gross output and value added.

The two tables show that the relative importance of the insurance industry to the financial sector fluctuated around 10%, depending on the year in which it is calculated and the measure that is used. This means that the insurance industry brings in about 10% of the business brought in by the financial sector as a whole, not counting real estate and "other financial services."

The insurance industry of Hong Kong has a long history. Starting when trades began to develop on the island in 1841, early insurance companies were organized as syndicates and were primarily in the business of marine, fire, and accident insurance.[2]

Table 3.1
Insurance Relative to the Financial Sector

(A) By Gross Output

Year	Finance (HK$ million)	Insurance Services (HK$ million)	Insurance / (Finance + Insurance) %
1980	11,726	1,125	8.75
1981	16,056	1,689	9.52
1982	18,606	1,853	9.06
1983	19,701	2,163	9.89
1984	21,792	2,265	9.42
1985	22,281	2,851	11.34
1986	27,624	3,208	10.40
1987	36,048	4,013	10.02
1988	40,249	5,104	11.25
1989	46,966	6,166	11.61
1990	55,851	6,910	11.01
1991	78,945	8,224	9.43
1992	95,017	9,806	9.35
1993	113,269	12,764	10.13

(B) By Value Added

Year	Finance (HK$ million)	Insurance Services (HK$ million)	Insurance / (Finance + Insurance) %
1980	8,760	869	9.02
1981	11,487	1,280	10.03
1982	12,926	1,349	9.45
1983	13,103	1,527	10.44
1984	14,177	1,631	10.32
1985	14,278	2,005	12.31
1986	18,362	2,226	10.81
1987	23,767	2,827	10.63
1988	26,057	3,560	12.02
1989	29,781	4,269	12.54
1990	34,600	4,555	11.63
1991	54,142	5,418	9.10
1992	69,602	6,609	8.67
1993	83,272	9,201	9.95

Source: Provided directly by the Census & Statistics Department, Hong Kong, 21 December 1995.

Note: Value added equals compensation of employee plus gross operating surplus.

Hong Kong has since evolved into an important Asian insurance centre. A rough count of the big players of the world suggests that as of 1994, twenty out of the fifty largest insurance companies in the world have branches or subsidiaries in Hong Kong.[3] (A list of the world's top fifty companies can be found in Appendix A.) Most of this rapid growth, especially in the area of life insurance, has been recent. This chapter highlights some of the important features of Hong Kong's insurance industry.[4]

Growth Rates and Inter-country Comparisons

The growth rate of the insurance industry in Hong Kong has been phenomenal in recent years. The total gross premium of the industry has increased at an average rate of 16.16% since 1983, a rate roughly comparable to the GDP growth rate of 15% during the same period.[5] In 1994 total gross premiums for the industry represented about 3.8% of the territory's gross domestic product.[6]

In spite of its high growth rate, Hong Kong's insurance industry cannot be considered particularly advanced as compared with that of OECD countries. In 1993 Hong Kong's insurance density (direct gross premium divided by the population size) was US$597, as compared with the OECD average of US$1,621. Hong Kong's insurance density is comparable to that of Finland, Italy, New Zealand, and Spain, but is far below that of countries such as Japan, Switzerland, the U.K. and the U.S., which have densities exceeding US$2,000. The penetration ratio (Direct Gross Premium divided by GDP) in Hong Kong was 3.15 in 1993, as compared with the OECD average of 8.16. Hong Kong's figure is comparable to that of countries such as Iceland, Italy, New Zealand, and Portugal; though coming close to Canada's figure of 4.49, the penetration ratio is far below that of the U.K. and the U.S., each of which has a penetration ratio that exceeds 10.

Table 3.2 compares a few characteristics of the insurance market in Hong Kong with those of the markets in OECD countries, using 1993 statistics as the basis for comparison. Aside from the density and the penetration ratio referred to in the

Table 3.2

Hong Kong's Insurance Industry Compared with OECD Countries

	Density Direct Gross Premium / Population (US$)	Penetration Ratio Direct Gross Premium/ GDP (%)	Life Insurance Share (%)	Productivity Direct Gross Premium / Employee US$	Retention Ratio (%)	Foreign Companies' Market Share (%)
Australia	1,444	9.05	59.09	—	87.69	—
Austria	1,258	5.52	31.57	304,649	83.73	33.82
Belgium	1,098	5.22	31.85	407,089	86.04	—
Canada	853	4.49	38.44	—	84.66	28.72
Denmark	1,384	5.28	44.89	48,962	87.95	7.65
Finland	491	3.97	18.37	210,767	90.38	—
France	1,656	7.63	55.21	782,979	91.52	—
Germany	1,485	6.31	35.46	470,748	80.92	11.33
Greece	141	2.00	46.30	73,215	78.41	33.00
Iceland	744	3.17	3.05	449,920	66.45	3.38
Ireland	1,216	9.08	56.58	429,236	84.36	—
Italy	570	3.22	30.56	664,443	81.36	—
Japan	2,921	8.64	73.32	560,551	89.16	2.66
Luxembourg	1,388	4.22	31.95	436,543	—	—
Mexico	63	4.60	32.61	287,744	79.80	—
Netherlands	1,537	7.61	51.62	333,666	88.27	22.85
New Zealand	391	3.11	46.94	—	91.36	—
Norway	1,318	5.50	37.29	488,244	84.46	1.77
Portugal	332	3.83	31.06	224,658	89.90	28.78
Spain	556	4.54	35.48	487,543	87.55	12.23
Sweden	1,309	6.16	48.86	285,199	—	0.00
Switzerland	3,099	9.26	41.81	577,275	86.63	2.78
Turkey	26	0.88	14.45	259,798	85.78	4.88
U.K.	2,103	12.92	58.66	454,213	87.75	—
U.S.	2,496	10.28	38.23	423,981	89.90	15.15
UE12	1,277	6.87	46.26	493,791	86.00	—
OECD	1,621	8.16	48.99	468,025	88.00	—
Hong Kong	597.32	3.07	48.3*	189,818	73.8	55**

Source : *Insurance Statistics Yearbook 1986–1993,* 1995 Edition, OECD. Statistics from Hong Kong compiled from *Estimates of Gross Domestic Product 1961–1994,* March 1995, *Survey of Storage, Communication, Financing, Insurance & Business Services, 1982–1993,* Census & Statistics Department, Hong Kong.

Notes : EU12 consists of the twelve countries of the EEC in 1993.
OECD stands for Organization for Economic Cooperation and Development.
Exchange rate: US$1=HK$7.8.

* Calculated based on Commissioner's Annual Report 1993.

** Calculated based on number of companies rather than total gross premium.

previous paragraph, measures of productivity (direct gross premium per employee) and retention ratio (net premium divided by gross premium) are low compared with OECD averages. The only figure higher than the OECD average is the foreign companies' market share, which is estimated to be 55% (counted by number of firms).[7] The aggregate insurance premium and its composition over time reflect many factors, including demand and supply, entry factors, accident rates, and, expenses and marketing efforts.

Composition of the Insurance Sector

A decomposition of the insurance industry into the two broad categories of life and general insurance (life versus non-life insurance) reveals a difference between the two sectors. The life insurance sector experienced more rapid growth during the period than did the general insurance sector. The average growth rate of gross premium in general insurance was 12%, whereas the comparable figure for life insurance was 34.01%.[8] The pattern is consistent with the rapid increase in the standard of living in the area during this period. As one can imagine, the demand for life insurance and its use as a savings component of a person's financial portfolio is likely to increase as standard of living improves. The demand for general insurance, to the extent that it largely insures against goods and properties, is driven more by general business activities than by standard of living.[9] A more rigorous proof of this assertion would require that a distinction be made between various "human capital"-related components, such as health and some proportion of accident insurance, and other, more property-related components, of general insurance. Nevertheless, even in the absence of such a distinction, the higher growth rate of the life insurance sector of Hong Kong relative to that of the general insurance sector is indisputable. In fact, unlike the overall insurance picture provided in the last section, which reveals statistics much lower than those of the OECD average, the life insurance share in Hong Kong (defined as the ratio of gross life insurance premium

Table 3.3
Composition of General Insurance Business in Hong Kong, 1993

	Earned Premium (EP)	Net Commissions Payable / (Receivable)		Management Expenses		Unexpired Risks Adjustment		Net Claims Incurred		Underwriting Profit/(Loss)	
Classes of Business	$m	$m	% of EP	$m	% of EP	$m	% of EP	$m	% of EP	$m	% of EP
Accident & Health	1,392.9	232.1	16.7	218.7	15.7	3.6	0.3	876.3	62.9	62.2	4.5
	1,482.1	256.7	17.3	227.7	15.4	3.9	0.3	936.7	63.2	57.1	3.9
Motor Vehicle	2,595.3	481.0	18.5	278.9	10.7	10.1	0.4	1,262.6	48.6	562.7	21.7
	2,998.5	577.5	19.3	315.9	10.5	10.7	0.4	1,534.4	51.2	560.0	18.7
Aircraft	0.0	(0.1)	–	0.2	–	(0.1)	–	0.0	–	0.0	–
	13.8	1.6	11.6	0.3	2.2	(0.1)	(0.7)	40.3	292.0	(28.3)	(205.1)
Ships	79.2	(19.4)	(24.5)	37.9	47.9	(1.0)	(1.3)	62.3	78.7	(0.6)	(0.8)
	158.5	(10.5)	(6.6)	47.7	30.1	(0.6)	(0.4)	155.5	98.1	(33.6)	(21.2)
Goods in Transit	696.6	140.2	20.1	142.6	20.5	7.2	1.0	213.3	213.3	193.3	27.7
	896.0	189.6	21.2	161.6	18.0	5.4	0.6	336.2	37.5	203.2	22.7
Property Damage	1,155.1	404.6	35.0	267.5	23.2	4.9	0.4	233.6	20.2	244.5	21.2
	2,188.7	797.2	36.4	346.7	15.8	(8.7)	(0.4)	863.8	39.5	189.7	8.7
General Liability	1,456.4	522.3	35.9	222.6	15.3	46.7	3.2	958.2	65.8	(293.4)	(20.1)
	1,655.5	573.5	34.6	241.8	14.6	46.3	2.8	1,162.9	70.2	(369.0)	(22.3)
Pecuniary Loss	68.8	12.4	18.0	16.8	24.4	1.4	2.0	8.2	11.9	30.0	43.6
	91.4	17.6	19.3	21.1	23.1	1.4	1.5	16.5	18.1	34.8	38.1
Nonproportional Treaty	n.a.	n.a.	n.a.	n.a.	n.a.	n.a.	n.a.	n.a.	n.a.	n.a.	n.a.
	61.2	6.1	10.0	1.3	2.1	0.0	0.0	68.7	112.3	(14.9)	(24.3)
Proportional Treaty	n.a.	n.a.	n.a.	n.a.	n.a.	n.a.	n.a.	n.a.	n.a.	n.a.	n.a.
	401.2	153.7	38.3	15.7	3.9	0.0	0.0	183.1	45.6	48.7	12.1
Overall	7,444.3	1,773.1	23.8	1,185.2	15.9	72.8	1.0	3,614.5	48.6	798.7	10.7
	9,946.9	2,563.0	25.8	1,379.8	13.9	58.3	0.6	5,298.1	53.3	647.7	6.5

Source: Office of the Commissioner of Insurance and the Registrar of Occupational Retirement Schemes, Hong Kong, *Annual Report 1994*, Figures 27 and 28, pp. 31–32.

Notes: The upper figure in each entry is direct business. The lower figure in each entry is direct and reinsurance inward business.
$m stands for HK$ million, EP = earned premium.

divided by total premium) is about the same as that of the average of all OECD countries.

General Insurance

Further decomposition of the general (non-life) and the long term (life) insurance sectors of Hong Kong reveals the types of insurance that are popular in Hong Kong. Table 3.3 gives the market shares of various types of general insurance in 1993. Property damage

Table 3.4
Overall Results for Hong Kong General Insurance Business

	1992 $m	1993 $m	1994 $m
Gross Premiums	14,181.7	17,081.9	19,736.7
Net Premiums	9,068.0	10,594.2	12,370.6
Technical Reserves	7,795.7	9,685.1	12,224.8
Underwriting Results:			
Earned Premiums	8,372.2	9,946.9	11,631.1
Commission Payable	4,161.2	4,529.0	4,859.5
Commission Receivable	1,655.4	1,966.0	2,033.4
Management Expenses	1,222.4	1,379.8	1,624.9
Unexpired Risks Adjustment	16.0	58.3	(8.8)
Net Claims Incurred	4,640.9	5,298.1	6,070.4
Underwriting Profit / (Loss)	(12.9)	647.7	1,118.5
Percentages and Ratios:	%	%	%
Growth of Gross Premiums	26.1	20.5	15.5
Retention Ratio	63.9	62.0	62.7
Commission Payable Ratio	29.3	26.5	24.6
Net Claims Incurred Ratio	55.4	53.3	52.2
Underwriting Margin	(0.2)	6.5	9.6
Technical Reserves Ratio*	86.0	91.4	98.8

Source: Office of the Commissioner of Insurance and the Registrar of Occupational Retirement Schemes, Hong Kong, *Annual Report* 1995, Figure 4.1.
*Note: Technical Reserves Ratio — Technical Reserves expressed as a percentage of net premiums.
$m stands for HK$ million.

business, motor vehicle, and general liability are the three prominent types of insurance on this list. Property damage insurance business ranked highest among the three in terms of total gross premium. In 1994 it accounted for 27% of total gross premium. The second-largest class was motor vehicle insurance, which amounted to 21% of the total gross premium of general insurance in the same year. The ranking changes slightly in net premium terms. The motor vehicle sector occupies the largest market share of 25%, followed by property damage and general

Table 3.5

Voluntary Termination Rate

Non-linked	Policy 1st Year		2nd Policy Year		3rd Policy Year		Overall			
	With Profits	Without Profits	With Profits	Without Profits	With Profits	Without Profits	1991	1992	1993	1994
	%	%	%	%	%	%	%	%	%	%
Whole Life*	18.4	19.2	6.6	16.4	4.8	7.2	12.6	10.5	9.1	8.8
Endowment	18.2	22.4	9.8	10.2	6.7	8.5	10.5	12.4	10.3	9.7
All Policies**	18.3	22.0	7.0	16.3	5.1	11.0	12.5	11.0	10.0	10.4

Linked of Insurance	Policy 1st Year	2nd Policy Year	3rd Policy Year and After	Overall			
				1991	1992	1993	1994
	%	%	%	%	%	%	%
Whole Life*	31.8	16.1	7.3	5.7	9.5	10.4	15.4
Endowment	6.7	8.3	4.3	9.3	11.7	8.4	5.9
All Policies**	20.0	13.3	6.2	7.0	10.5	9.6	11.6

Source: Office of the Commissioner of Insurance and the Registrar of Occupational Retirement Schemes, Hong Kong, *Annual Report* 1995, Figure 5.5.

Note: * Whole Life represents whole life and anticipated endowment insurance.
** All policies include term policies and others.

Table 3.6

Voluntary Termination Rate — Ordinary Policies in Force in the U.S.

Year	1978	1979	1980	1981	1982	1983	1984	1985
	%	%	%	%	%	%	%	%
Policies In Force Less Than 2 Years	19.6	21.0	22.4	23.5	24.4	25.1	23.0	20.9
Policies In Force 2 Years or More	4.6	5.1	5.8	6.6	7.6	8.6	9.6	10.3
All Policies In Force	6.6	7.2	8.1	8.9	10.0	11.1	11.9	12.3

Year	1986	1987	1988	1989	1990	1991	1992	1993
	%	%	%	%	%	%	%	%
Policies In Force Less Than 2 Years	21.7	20.5	19.8	18.6	19.0	19.4	18.3	17.4
Policies In Force 2 Years or More	9.0	8.3	7.0	6.7	6.6	6.5	6.4	5.8
All Policies In Force	11.1	10.2	9.3	8.8	8.7	8.6	8.3	7.6

Source : American Council of Life Insurance, *Life Insurance Fact Book*, 1994, p. 67.

liability, with shares of 23% and 20%, respectively.[10]

Table 3.4 gives the overall results for the general insurance business in Hong Kong from 1992–1994. The technical reserves ratio is close to 99%, with an overall net claims incurred ratio of 52.2%. With the exception of motor vehicle and employee compensation insurance, the overall underwriting margin is moderate. In 1994, aircraft, ships and employee compensation business recorded underwriting losses whereas motor business recorded a profit.

Life Insurance

Much in the way that insurance is classified in the U.S., or in the way in which Canadian economies divide life insurance policies into permanent life insurance (such as whole, universal, and variable life) and temporary insurance (such as term), the life insurance market in Hong Kong can be divided into two broad categories of linked and non-linked long-term businesses. Linked businesses are permanent businesses with an investment component that is controlled in some dimension by the policyholders themselves — usually in terms of the percentage of portfolio they wish to hold in stocks versus bonds or other investment instruments. Non-linked businesses have no direct investment component partially or wholly controlled by the policyholders, but they can be "with profits" (participating) or "without profits" (non-participating). In the former case, the insurance company will in effect act as the investment representative for the policyholders. With dividends being paid out of the investment income, a policyholder is sharing in the profit of the insurance company without actually participating as he does in the case of linked long-term business.

Non-linked long-term business can be further divided into five categories: whole life, anticipated endowment, endowment, terms, and others. The simplest form of life insurance is term insurance, which is temporary in the sense that it is for a period of time, and has to be renewed when the contract expires. It contains no saving components. Endowment is life insurance payable to the policyholder, if living, on the maturity date stated in the policy, or

Table 3.7

Composition of Long-term Insurance Business in Hong Kong, 1993

Type of Insurance	Non-Linked Long-Term Business				Linked Long-Term Business	
	New Business		Business In Force		New Business	Business In Force
	With Profit	Without Profit	With Profit	Without Profit		
No. of Policies						
Whole Life	255,205 (74.31%)	14,227 (7.63%)	1,172,148 (81.53%)	56,438 (7.62%)	14,325 (64.79%)	40,301 (62.45%)
Anticipated Endowment	54,687 (15.92%)	67,528 (36.22%)	84,244 (5.86%)	379,517 (51.22%)	7,739 (35.00%)	24,047 (37.27%)
Endowment	33,424 (9.73%)	11,763 (6.31%)	181,100 (12.60%)	20,183 (2.72%)	N.A.	N.A.
Term	3 (0.00%)	29,931 (16.05%)	36 (0.00%)	90,613 (12.23%)	N.A.	N.A.
Others	108 (0.03%)	62,994 (33.79%)	171 (0.01%)	194,179 (26.21%)	181 (0.28%)	
Total	343,427	186,443	1,437,699	740,930	22,109	64,529
Office Premiums						
Whole Life	1,117.30 (64.75%)	52.9 (4.91%)	4,643.10 (73.56%)	217.9 (5.73%)	950 (87.72%)	399.1 (67.94%)
Anticipated Endowment	351.3 (20.36%)	314.6 (29.20%)	534.6 (8.47%)	1,657.90 (43.63%)	130 (12.00%)	188.3 (32.06%)
Endowment	251.9 (14.60%)	98.4 (9.13%)	949.9 (15.05%)	139.6 (3.67%)	N.A.	N.A.
Term	0 (0.00%)	127.6 (11.84%)	0.4 (0.01%)	182.3 (4.80%)	N.A.	N.A.
Others	5.1 (0.30%)	483.8 (44.91%)	184.2 (2.92%)	1,602.10 (42.16%)		
Total	1,725.60	1,077.30	6,312.20	3,799.80	1,083	587.4

Type of Insurance	Non-Linked Long-Term Business				Linked Long-Term Business	
	New Business		Business In Force		New Business	Business In Force
	With Profit	Without Profit	With Profit	Without Profit		
Sums Assured						
Whole Life	N.A.	N.A.	338,899.60 (78.99%)	25,270.30 (7.82%)	N.A.	N.A.
Anticipated Endowment	N.A.	N.A.	19,927.20 (4.64%)	42,109.70 (13.03%)	N.A.	N.A.
Endowment	N.A.	N.A.	49,989.20 (11.65%)	6,643.90 (2.06%)	N.A.	N.A.
Term	N.A.	N.A.	43.5 (0.01%)	54,026.40 (16.72%)	N.A.	N.A.
Others	N.A.	N.A.	20,196.80 (4.71%)	195,107.40 (60.38%)	N.A.	N.A.
Total	N.A.	N.A.	429,056.30	323,157.70	N.A.	N.A.
Net Liability						
Whole Life	N.A.	N.A.	8,453.80 (70.64%)	603.3 (12.57%)	N.A.	3,699.30 (89.49%)
Anticipated Endowment	N.A.	N.A.	328.8 (2.75%)	2,809.90 (58.55%)	N.A.	423.4 (10.24%)
Endowment	N.A.	N.A.	2,903.10 (24.26%)	340.7 (7.10%)	N.A.	N.A.
Term	N.A.	N.A.	0.6 (0.01%)	251.5 (5.24%)	N.A.	N.A.
Others	N.A.	N.A.	281.7 (2.35%)	793.7 (16.54%)	N.A.	9.1 (0.22%)
Reserves	N.A.	N.A.	N.A.	N.A.	N.A.	2.1 (0.05%)
Total	N.A.	N.A.	11,968.00	4,799.10	N.A.	4,133.90

Source: Office of The Commissioner of Insurance And The Registrar of Occupational Retirement Schemes, *Annual Report 1994.*
Figures are in HK$ million, percentages are expressed in parentheses.

Table 3.8
Composition of Long-Term Insurance Business in Hong Kong (Business in Force)

Composition	Total	Whole Life %	Anticipated Endowment %	Endowment %	Term %	Others %
No. of Policies	2,243,158	56.57	20.7	10.05	4.04	8.67
Office Premiums ($m)	10,699	49.2	20.5	11.9	1.71	16.70
Sums Assured ($m)	752,214	48.41	8.25	7.53	7.19	28.62

Source: Reconstructed from Figure 38 (p. 40) of *Annual Report 1994*, Office of Commissioner of Insurance and the Registrar of Occupational Retirement Scheme.
$m stands for HK$ million.

Table 3.9
Analysis of Ordinary Life Insurance Purchases in the U.S.

Type of Policy	% of Policies 1983	% of Policies 1993	% of Face Amount 1983	% of Face Amount 1993
Whole Life – continuous pay	33	36	17	18
Whole Life – continuous pay, term rider	2	1	2	2
Whole Life – limited pay	9	10	2	2
Modified Life	4	1	3	1
Level Term and Modified Term	21	21	42	40
Decreasing Term	3	1	2	1
Policies with Family Plan	7	7	6	4
Enhancement	1	2	1	3
Universal Life	14	10	21	10
Variable Life	2	2	1	5
Variable-Universal Life	–	8	–	12
Other Combined Coverage	4	1	3	2
Total	100	100	100	100

Source: American Council of Life Insurance, *Life Insurance Fact Book*, 1994, p.12.
Note: Figures exclude credit life insurance and single premium policies

to a beneficiary if the insured dies prior to that date. Anticipated endowment is similar to a whole life, but pays pre-specified lump sums to a policyholder at periodical intervals. Finally, the most popular form of insurance is whole life, which is life insurance payable to a beneficiary upon the death of the insured, whenever that occurs.

A good measure of the quality of the long-term products is the voluntary termination rate. Table 3.5 provides the voluntary termination rates of non-linked and linked products in Hong Kong. The overall voluntary termination rate of non-linked products (for policies over two years old) is 10.4%. Compared with the U.S. figure in Table 3.6, this figure is a little higher, but not much. In 1985, for example, the U.S. rate was as high as 10.3%. Policies less than two years old usually have a higher voluntary termination rate. This is the same in Hong Kong as it is in the U.S. Another way to measure long-term products offered in Hong Kong is to examine complaints filed through the Insurance Claims Complaints Board. In 1994 only nine out of sixty-two cases filed through the board were life product cases. Out of the nine, four had to do with the terms of the policy, and four had to do with nondisclosure.[11]

The distribution of these policies in 1993 by number, by office premiums, by sum assured, and by net liability is listed in Table 3.7. New business refers to the policies sold in that year. Business in force refers to the cumulative policies in existence as of 1993. Thus, in 1993, counting linked and non-linked policies, there were approximately 2,243,158 individual policies in force in Hong Kong. Dividing this figure by the total population of 5.92 million in Hong Kong in that year gives us a penetration rate of 37.89%. In other words, close to four out of ten persons in Hong Kong already have some life insurance.[12]

Out of the 2,243,158 individual policies in existence in Hong Kong, 4.04% are in the area of term insurance, 10% are in the area of endowment, 20.7% are in the area of anticipated endowment, and the majority (56.57%) are in the area of whole life.[13] In office premium terms, out of a total of HK$10,699.4 million, only 1.7% are in the area of term insurance. The percentages going to the other

Table 3.10
Relative Shares of Total Financial Intermediary, 1960–1993 (%)

	1960	1970	1980	1990	1993
Insurance companies					
Life insurance	19.6	15.3	11.5	12.5	13.0
Property and casualty	4.4	3.8	4.5	4.9	4.6
Pension funds					
Private	6.4	8.4	12.5	14.9	17.0
Public (state and local government)	3.3	4.6	4.9	6.7	7.7
Finance companies	4.7	4.9	5.1	5.6	4.8
Mutual funds					
Stock and bond	2.9	3.6	1.7	5.9	11.1
Money market	0.0	0.0	1.9	4.6	4.1
Depository institutions (banks)					
Commercial banks	38.6	38.5	36.7	30.4	28.1
S&Ls and mutual savings banks	19.0	19.4	19.6	12.5	7.5
Credit unions	1.1	1.4	1.6	2.0	2.1
Total	100.0	100.0	100.0	100.0	100.0

Source: Frederic S. Mishkin (1995), *Financial Markets, Institutions, And Money*, HarperCollins College Publishers.

categories are similar to those when the number of policies are used. In sums assured terms, the percentage in term insurance is at 7.19%. Term insurance accounts for only a small percentage of the life insurance products sold in Hong Kong. The tabulation of these percentages is summarized in Table 3.8.

The figures are not exactly parallel to those in the U.S., as life insurance products are defined slightly differently there. Nevertheless, Table 3.9 provides a broad view for the purpose of comparison. In 1993, traditional whole life insurance and its variations represented the largest portion of sales in the U.S., with a penetration rate of 78%, and 48% of all policies sold belonging to that category. Universal and variable sales accounted for 20% of the new policies sold, and term insurance accounted for 22%.[14] Term insurance occupied a 21% total in terms of number of policies, and much more (40%) in terms of the face amount. The

Table 3.11

Composition of Long-Term Insurance Business in Force in Hong Kong, 1993

Composition	Total	Individual Life %	Group Life %	Annuity %	Permanent Health %	Retirement Schemes %
No. of policies	2,325,530	96.46	0.33	0.01	2.82	0.39
Office premiums ($m)	15,490	69.07	2.85	0.00	0.37	27.71
Net liability ($m)	43,503	48.65	0.67	0.11	0.13	50.44

Source: Reconstructed from Figure 5.1 (p. 24) of *Annual Report 1995*, Office of the Commissioner of Insurance and the Registrar of Occupational Retirement Schemes, Hong Kong.
$m stands for HK$ million.

popularity of term insurance in the U.S. is no doubt due to the availability of retirement pension plans. Individuals in the U.S. who wish to participate in long-term savings plans will do so via pension funds, leaving life insurance purely for risk protection in the form of term insurance. As Table 3.10 indicates, insurance companies' assets, as a percentage of all financial assets in the U.S., were higher than were those of the pension funds in the 1960s, but the trend has reversed in the 1990s.

Retirement schemes in Hong Kong are much less extensive than are those in the U.S. Table 3.11 reveals this pattern. Retirement schemes occupy less than 1% of the total number of insurance policies in Hong Kong, though in terms of office premiums and net liability, they occupy 27.71% and 50.44%, respectively.[15] Life insurance as a competing channel of savings in the economy occupied roughly 16.62% of total saving in Hong Kong in 1994, marking a gradual increase from 9.03% in 1982. Insurance sector value added as a percentage of the value added of other financial services in the region ranged between 8% and 12% from 1983 to 1993, as was described at the beginning of this chapter.

Another interesting observation about life insurance in Hong Kong is that the extent of profit participation is quite large in whole life policy. Again, using Table 3.7 as an indicator, lumping "with

Table 3.12

Number of Companies Authorized by Class of Insurance Business and by Country of Incorporation as of June 1994

Class of insurance business authorized		Number of companies authorized by country of incorporation				
Class	Description	Hong Kong	UK	US	Others	Total
	Classes of long-term business					
A	Life and annuity	15	8	7	27	57
B	Marriage and birth	5	2	1	3	11
C	Linked long term	6	4	1	14	25
D	Permanent health	9	5	3	12	29
E	Tontines	5	–	1	2	8
F	Capital redemption	5	2	1	3	11
G	Retirement scheme management category I	3	–	–	2	5
H	Retirement scheme management category II	–	–	–	–	0
I	Retirement scheme management category III	4	3	–	3	10
1	Accident	87	21	14	44	166
2	Sickness	68	17	13	35	133
3	Land vehicles	58	16	13	34	121
4	Railway rolling stock	79	14	13	44	150
5	Aircraft	35	14	11	26	86
6	Ships	79	16	12	43	150
7	Goods in transit	82	21	13	46	162
8	Fire and natural forces	85	17	14	41	157
9	Damage to property	84	17	14	41	156
10	Motor vehicle liability	57	13	12	33	115
11	Aircraft liability	40	13	11	26	90
12	Liability for ships	78	16	11	43	148
13	General liability	80	17	12	40	149
14	Credit	51	11	10	24	96
15	Suretyship	73	19	11	41	144
16	Miscellaneous financial loss	71	16	13	36	136
17	Legal expenses	46	13	11	24	94
Average number of classes of insurance business authorized per insurer		11.70	10.17	10.57	9.28	10.61

Source: HongkongBank, *The Insurance Industry of Hong Kong,* 1994, Table 2, p.15.

profit" non-linked business with linked business as one category representing variable pay-off, 95.5% of whole life policies had variable pay-off, while the corresponding figures for endowment and anticipated endowment were 90% and 22.22%, respectively. The smaller percentage of variable pay-off policies in the category of anticipated endowment is puzzling. Indeed, the ratio of whole life to anticipated endowment policies in the category of non-linked policies with profits was about 14 to 1, whereas the comparable figure for policies without profits was about 1 to 7.[16]

Number of Firms

An interesting fact about the insurance industry in Hong Kong is that a large number of firms are crowded into a small place. Indeed, Hong Kong has the highest number of authorized insurance companies in Asia. Among the 223 authorized insurers in the territory in 1995, 22 were reinsurers, of which 6 were incorporated locally and 16 were branch offices of overseas companies. Table 3.12 gives a breakdown of the number of authorized insurer in each category of business in 1994. For general insurance, the average number of firms in each category was around 100. For long-term business, the number is smaller. For life insurance, the registered number is 57.

A large number of firms does not necessarily mean a low concentration ratio. Although competition among insurance companies in Hong Kong is quite severe, the life insurance industry is dominated by three companies — AIA, National Mutual, and Manual Life, which together allegedly control about 75% of the market. This alone is not sufficient to suggest that the companies have "market power" over their competitors, however. In fact, the general impression in the industry is that it seems quite saturated in terms of the number of insurance companies. The number of establishments as provided in Table B.6 in Appendix B shows a somewhat erratic pattern over time. Establishments in Table B.6 are counted by the survey conducted by the Department of Census and Statistics. The interesting thing about this pattern is that the survey

Table 3.13

Principal Statistics for All Establishments by Major Industry Group, Industry Group and Income and Receipts, 1993

Income and Receipts (HK$ thousand)	< 500	500 to 999	1,000 to 4,999	5000 to 9,999	10,000 to 19,999	20,000 to 49,999	50,000+	Total
General insurers								
Number of Establishment	3	5	13	5	14	23	58	122
No of Persons Engaged	16	0	23	21	107	418	3608	4,193
No of Employees	16	0	23	21	107	418	3608	4,193
Compensation of Employees	*	725	3,924	*	23,438	*	805,575	927,812
Operating Expenses	*	382	11,629	*	21,960	*	634,247	753,699
Net Premium	*	2,241	3,018	*	59,361	*	5,888,764	6,111,701
Net Claims	*	1,630	9,088	*	43,052	*	3,934,733	4,370,675
Funds and Reserves	*	33,681	15,864	*	374,288	*	9,207.705	10,325,350
Income and Receipts	*	4739	19614	*	203,301	*	13,033,965	13,902,595
Gross Additions to Fixed Assets	*	–8	–19	*	2,350	*	58,871	79,080
Floor Area (sq.m.)	*	0	605	*	1829	*	49,950	62,762
Life insurers								
No of Establishment	4	3	5	2	3	1	30	50
No of Persons Engaged	4	2	7		63	6	14,337	14433
No of Employees	4	2	7	13	63	6	14,337	14433
Compensation of Employees	*	529	3,349	13	15,738	*	3,269,876	3,295,376
Operating Expenses	*	348	3,452	*	18,882	*	1,301,731	1,333,757
Net Premium	*	504	7,138	*	16,668	*	13,790,999	13,823,320
Net Claims	*	3,993	7,845	*	2,250	*	6,025,480	6,042,518
Funds and Reserves	*	7,491	26,698	*	161,718	*	40,958,281	41,184,346
Income and Receipts	*	1,935	10,766	*	38,988	*	18,309,114	18,398,897
Gross Additions to Fixed Assets	*	26	1,034	*	5,246	*	138,656	144,967
Floor Area (sq.m.)	*	27	303	*	2,499	*	116,055	119,336

Source: Census and Statistics Department, Hong Kong, *Report on 1993 Survey of Storage, Communication, Financing, Insurance & Business Services*, Table 3.3, pp.47–48.

*Note: Data not released in order to safeguard confidentiality of information provided by individual firm.

number of establishments does not increase as market size increases. If anything, there seems to be a decreasing trend, suggesting the possibility of scale economies.

The number of establishments in Hong Kong seems to be lower than the number of registered companies. This discrepancy could reflect three things. First, a registered insurer may rely entirely on independent agents and brokers to sell insurance. Keeping a big local office is not necessary. Second, a parent company might act as a holding company of several subsidiaries. Only the subsidiaries, and not the holding company, have business transactions. Third, a registered insurer can be dormant and non-operating.

Distribution of Firms

Table 3.13 from the Census Statistics provides a broad view of the distribution of the 172 insurance establishments in Hong Kong in 1993. For general insurance, the top fifty insurers had an annual income and receipts of more than HK$50 million, and they employed an average of sixty-two people per establishment. Smaller companies had an income and receipts of less than HK$500,000. There are three companies in this category, each of which employed about five people. Life insurers firms were generally larger. Thirty out of the fifty life insurers had an annual income and receipts of more than HK$50 million. However, there are also some extremely small companies in this category. Four such establishments had an annual income and receipts of less than HK$500,000 and employed only one person each. Twelve of the life insurers earned less than HK$5 million in 1993.

Investment Philosophy

The investment philosophy of Hong Kong insurance companies can be considered conservative. Some have in-house investment departments, but others rely on outside fund managers to make their investment decisions. The high proportion of "foreign insurers" in the industry may lead to the speculation that a large

Table 3.14
Investment, 1987–92

Investments	1992 HK$ m	92/91 %	91/90 %	90/89 %	89/88 %	88/87 %	87/86 %
General insurers (112)							
Financial Assets	10,008	9.1	–6.8	14.5	20.9	10.6	17.1
Fixed Assets	188	3.9	–11.6	–0.1	12.0	–4.3	41.5
Total	10,196	9.0	–6.9	14.2	20.7	10.2	17.6
Life insurers (49)							
Financial Assets	30,297	12.7	68.3	20.0	12.9	1.1	15.0
Fixed Assets	144	21.1	–23.8	27.7	8.9	–3.8	–0.9
Total	30,442	12.8	67.4	20.1	20.1	1.1	14.8
Total (161)							
Financial Assets	40,305	11.8	39.7	17.9	15.9	4.5	15.7
Fixed Assets	332	10.7	–16.9	10.6	10.9	–4.1	21.8
Total	40,638	11.8	38.9	17.8	15.9	4.4	15.8

Source: HongkongBank, *The Insurance Industry of Hong Kong,* 1995, Table 13, p. 59.
Notes : (1) Figures in parentheses are the number of establishments included in the 1992 survey.
(2) The term "insurers" refers to both insurers and reinsurers.

portion of the funds were invested outside Hong Kong. No public statistics from which to ascertain whether or not this is true are readily available at this point. However, even if offshore investment is high, this will not necessarily jeopardize the stability of the system. As long as insurers have a sufficient solvency margin, investment risks will already have been captured in terms of the calculation of the cushion. Indeed, in the recent history of the industry, though some insurance companies have experienced financial difficulties, no insurance contracts have ever been dishonoured outright.[17] The asset distribution of insurance companies in aggregate and by selected sample of observation is reported in Tables 3.14 and 3.15, respectively. Some recent changes in regulations concerning types of investment will be addressed in the next chapter.

Table 3.15
Distribution of Assets, 1984–92

	1992 (50) %	1991 (50) %	1990 (44) %	1989 (44) %	1988 (44) %	1987 (44) %	1986 (44) %	1985 (45) %	1984 (46) %
Investment in related companies	3.8	3.6	4.8	5.6	5.9	5.1	5.3	4.5	6.0
Loans and mortgages	17.0	18.0	18.3	16.1	15.5	14.0	14.1	15.3	15.6
Stocks, shares and bonds	40.0	33.5	38.9	43.0	44.9	45.8	46.4	41.9	36.8
Amounts due from related companies	4.4	8.2	3.2	3.4	3.0	3.6	4.1	4.0	3.0
Deposits and cash balances	23.3	26.3	24.5	19.6	19.6	20.7	19.2	20.5	23.1
Fixed and call deposits	20.1	24.1	21.8	17.6	16.7	17.6	17.0	18.9	19.0
Cash and bank balances	2.4	1.3	0.9	2.1	3.0	3.1	2.1	1.6	1.5
Property and fixed assets	4.3	3.0	2.8	2.7	2.8	3.0	2.8	3.0	2.8
Property	3.6	2.4	2.1	2.1	2.3	2.5	2.3	2.5	2.2
Other fixed assets	0.7	0.6	0.7	0.5	0.5	0.5	0.5	0.5	0.5
Other assets	7.3	7.4	7.6	9.7	8.2	7.8	8.2	10.9	13.2
Total assets	100.0	100.0	100.0	100.0	100.0	100.0	100.0	100.0	100.0

Source: HongkongBank, *The Insurance Industry of Hong Kong,* 1995, Table 36, p.114.
Notes: (1) Figures in parentheses refer to the number of companies included in this study.
(2) Numbers may not add up to totals since the breakdowns are not available for some insurers.

Profitability

Profitability studies have been performed in Wong (1991) and also in an annual survey of the industry by The Hongkong and Shanghai Banking Corporation. In the 1980s insurance underwriting in Hong Kong compared favourably with that of other international markets. For general insurance, the estimated rates of return on shareholders' funds were 10.2%, 14.5%, and 10.6% in 1985, 1986, and 1987 respectively, based on a random sample.[18] The rough impression is that from 1988 to 1991 profits generally declined. The average rates of return of the industry were 11.2%, 7.7%, 9.3%, and 8% from 1998 to 1991.[19] Especially in the area of specialist reinsurers, the rate of return was negative in 1989–91.

The numbers derived are rough estimates, as insurance

companies of all types are lumped together in the calculation of the averages. Certainly, in the area of life insurance, the estimated rates of return are much more attractive. They have been estimated at 27%, 25%, 49.7%, and 32% in 1988, 1989, 1990, and 1991, respectively. For the reported rate of return in 1992, the average rate was as high as 55.1% (based on a small sample of only four companies). Having adjusted by also counting composite insurers, the estimate falls to a more reasonable level of 8.7%.[20]

General Characteristics of the Sales Force in Hong Kong

The summary statistics of the insurance sales force are shown in the third category of Table 3.16. More than half of the establishments are small businesses with a reported annual income and receipts of less than HK$500,000 (US$64,103), occupying an office area of just 11.2 square metres (approximately 120 square feet). On the other end of the spectrum are four larger establishments, each with an annual income and receipts of over HK$50 million (US$6.41 million).

Another source of information of general characteristics of the Hong Kong sales force is the Vocational Training Council. Of the close to 30,000-strong force of insurance practitioners in Hong Kong, a large proportion are agents and salespeople. According to the statistics provided by the Insurance Training Board of the Council, summarized in the *1993 Manpower Survey* Report, out of a total of 11,256 people working in general insurance, 4,378 (39%) were classified as agents, and out of a total of 17,081 people working in life insurance, 12,805 (82%) were classified as agents.[21] Table 3.17 provides the total number of agents and the distribution of their monthly income in 1993. Monthly income used in the survey includes basic salary, overtime, bonuses, housing allowance, cost-of-living allowance, and meal allowance, and excludes payments in kind. June was used as the month during which to record the average commission income.[22] General and life insurance are reported separately. The survey canvassed 626

Table 3.16
Insurance Agents, Brokers and Other Insurance Services

Income and Receipts ($'000)	< 500	500 to 999	1,000 to 4,999	5000 to 9,999	10,000 to 19,999	20,000 to 49,999	550,000+	Total
No. of Establishment	1588	297	168	31	31	15	4	2,134
No. of Persons Engaged	2,377	782	1,069	399	711	692	504	6,494
No. of Employees	1,232	698	1,058	396	711	692	504	5,291
Compensation of Employees	80,407	77,906	160,766	95,251	132,963	162,846	139,737	846,877
Operating Expenses	154,069	68,916	172,843	82,230	78,198	112,602	73,935	742,793
Income and Receipts	286,732	189,378	410,239	231,171	356,636	430,260	297,788	2,202,205
Gross Additions to Fixed Assets	7,322	2,778	12,836	4,189	9,052	12,001	13,636	61,851
Floor Area (sq.m.)	17,791	7,210	10,975	5,011	8,355	8,346	7,302	64,990

Source: Census and Statistics Department, Hong Kong, *Report on 1993 Survey of Storage, Communication, Financing, Insurance & Business Services*, Table 3.3, pp. 47–48.

establishments, including 230 authorized insurers, 53 of their branches, 38 major insurance brokers, and 305 active insurance agencies, covering an estimated 90% of the insurance industry workforce.

The patterns exhibited in the table reveal the following: First, there are more than twice as many life insurance agents as there are general insurance agents in Hong Kong. In view of the fact that the gross premium of life insurance is lower than is that of general insurance, premium per agent (or output per agent) is less for life insurance than it is for general insurance. Second, the agent-to-manager/supervisor ratio is much higher for general insurance than it is for life insurance. There are 338 agents to one manager/supervisor in the general insurance industry, whereas the ratio is more like ten agents to one manager/supervisor in the life insurance industry. Third, among the respondents who reported their income, the median income of life insurance agents is higher than that of general insurance agents. Life insurance agents have a median monthly income of HK$15,000 to HK$20,000, while the median monthly income of general insurance agents is HK$7,000 to HK$10,000. Fourth, there are more life insurance agents than there are general insurance agents who are unwilling to report their

Table 3.17
The Distribution of Insurance Employees and Agents by Sector, by Job Level and by Total Monthly Income Range

Job Level	General Insurance Total Workforce: 11,256		Life Insurance Total Workforce: 17,081	
	Managerial/ Supervisory	Agents	Managerial/ Supervisory	Agents
Total number employed	13	4,378	1,203	12,805
$4,000 or below	2 (15.4)	57 (1.3)	–	– –
$4,001 – $7,000	1 (7.7)	165 (3.8)	–	18 (0.1)
$7,001 – $10,000	–	2,732 (62.2)	–	878 (6.9)
$10,001 – $15,000	6 (46.2)	663 (15.1)	2 (0.2)	753 (5.9)
$15,001 – $20,000	3 (23.0)	32 (0.7)	18 (1.5)	3,506 (27.4)
$20,001 – $25,000	1 (7.7)	16 (0.4)	13 (0.1)	13 (0.1)
$25,001 – $35,000	–	– –	41 (3.4)	1 –
$35,001 or above	–	10 (0.2)	388 (32.3)	– –
Unspecified	–	712 (16.3)	741 (61.6)	7,636 (59.6)

Source: Insurance Training Board, Vocational Training Council, *1993 Manpower Survey Report: Insurance Industry.*

monthly income. Of the life insurance agents surveyed, 59.6% did not specify their income, as compared to only 16.3% of the general insurance agents.

Life insurance agents' frequent failure to report their income can be further commented upon. Life insurance agents are quite individualistic, even though they are "managed". Successive layers of life insurance marketing management can also be broken down hierarchically into units and districts, with the former group acting under the latter group's supervision.[23] Above the agents are the assistant unit managers, the unit managers, and the senior unit managers. The marketing operation is to be supervised by a district manager. After amassing sufficient experience, a district manager can be promoted to senior district manager. Managers not only sell products themselves, but are also in charge of recruiting, training, and managing other agents. Managers receive a percentage of the commission of the agents they recruit. The income of an insurance company person with five years of experience can be as high as HK$1 million.[24] The experienced and successful manager can allegedly command an annual income of over HK$10 million.[25]

Summary

This chapter highlights the essential features of Hong Kong's insurance industry. The quantitative dimensions chosen for this description are those currently monitored by the government in public records. According to these measures, nothing about the industry indicates that the system needs an overhaul. Indeed, in spite of a slight divergence since 1983 from the laissez faire operating principle, the industry has continued to perform respectably.

Notes

1. *Estimates of Gross Domestic Product, 1961 to 1994*, Census and Statistics Department, Hong Kong, pp. 84-85.
2. Early insurance companies such as the China Insurance Company (later the Union Insurance Society of Canton), and the Hong Kong Fire Insurance Company Ltd. are well known names even today. See the early history of the industry in *Insurance Markets of the World*, The Swiss Reinsurance Company, Zurich, 1964, p. 435.
3. Base on Fortune Global 500, in terms of revenue for 1995, 27 out of the 50 largest insurance companies have operations in Hong Kong.
4. Aside from the annual reports provided by the Insurance Commissioner, descriptions of the Hong Kong insurance industry can be found in the Hongkong Bank's survey of the insurance industry, *The Insurance Industry of Hong* Kong. Additional information can be found in Wong (1991), Yip (1994), and a series of MBA theses at the University of Hong Kong and the Chinese University of Hong Kong.
5. Wong, ibid, estimated the growth rate to be slightly higher at 17.9% between 1981 and 1987. The average figure provided here is in Yip (ibid.) from 1983 to 1991. Recent figures were higher, at 20% in 1995, but fell in 1996.
6. Figure provided by Insurance Commissioner at the Emerging Asian Insurance Markets International summit, 25 March 1996. Related measures of the growth of the industry also reveal a similar pattern. In terms of employment size, technical funds and reserves, densities (premium as ratio of GDP and premium as ratio of population), penetration ratio, and claims and expenses, the industry revealed a consistent upward rising pattern since 1982. See Appendix B for a tabulation of these statistics.

7. Based on the figures provided by the Insurance Authority, 43% of 1995 gross premium in general insurance is from non-HK origin insurers. For long term business, insurers in Hong Kong wrote 2.3% and 3.1% of the total premium in 1994 and 1995 respectively.

8. The figures were given by the Insurance Authority calculation, from 1983 to 1995 Yip (1994) estimated 9.83% for the period between 1983 and 1991. Wong (1991) reported that the average annual growth rate of general insurance was 14.8% between 1981 and 1987, while that of life was 27.5% during the same period. Although the difference is smaller, it still shows the higher rate of the life sector.

9. This is the main argument in Chapter 2 of C. W. Yip's 1994 study. Four wage indexes have been used to measure the standard of living. Measures of general business activities include overseas merchandise trade, and private and government consumption. A high correlation between each measure and the demand for its respective insurance have been observed.

10. The composition prior to 1990 can be found in Yueng (1990) and Wong (1991), p. 149.

11. The Insurance Claims Complaints Board, *Annual Report*, *1994*, p. 11.

12. The figure can be compared with an independent survey conducted in this study in Chapter 6.

13. The total number of policies is obtained by adding total non-linked policy "with profits" types (1,437,699), non-linked policy "without profits" types (740,930), and linked policy (64,529).

14. *Life Insurance Fact Book,* p. 11.

15. Retirement scheme policies are group policies in nature and therefore the number of such policies is not comparable with the total number of policies which reflects mostly individual policies.

16. *Annual Report,* 1994, p. 40.

17. Failure of a company can be due to bankruptcy or voluntary liquidation. The information is based on an informal inquiry made to the Office of Insurance Commissioner.

18. Wong (1991), p. 147.

19. Yip (1994), pp. 91–95.

20. *The Insurance Industry of Hong Kong, 1995,* p. 5.

21. Based on Tables 1a and 1b of the *Report*, pp. 63–66.

22. *1993 Manpower Survey Report,* p. 12.

23. Article from *HK Economic Times*, 11 December 1995.

24. Article from *HK Economic Journal*, 5 December 1995.
25. Article from *HK Economic Times*, 11 December 1995.

CHAPTER 4

Regulatory Framework, Trends and Issues

The central piece of insurance legislation in Hong Kong is the *Insurance Companies Ordinance,* which is enforced and implemented by the Insurance Authority and the Commissioner of Insurance. The Office of the Commissioner of Insurance is under the Secretary for Financial Services who is under the Financial Secretary (see Figure 4.1). The Financial Services Branch of the government was previously the Monetary Affairs Branch (MAB) of the government, which was also in charge of the Office of the Commissioner of Banking. Since the forming of the Hong Kong Monetary Authority (HKMA) in 1993, banking supervision has been taken out of the MAB; whatever remained was renamed the Financial Services Branch which the insurance division is now under. This historical development may imply a gradual move towards autonomy for the Insurance Authority. Such a shift has benefits as well as costs.

The operation of the Insurance Authority has not yet been made autonomous. Under the existing regulatory framework, aside from the Financial Services Branch, those having a bearing on the workings of the Insurance Authority are the Governor, the Financial Secretary, and the Insurance Advisory Board.[1] For example, there is a right of appeal against certain decisions made by the Insurance Authority, such as the refusal of authorization (See Insurance Companies Ordinance, s(11), *Appeal against refusal of authorization under* s 8(2)). The governor also has the power to

Figure 4.1
Hong Kong Government Secretariat — Organization Chart

FINANCIAL SECRETARY	
Secretary for Works	❑ Architectural Services Department ❑ Civil Engineering Department ❑ Drainage Services ❑ Electrical & Mechanical Services Department ❑ New Airport Projects Co-ordination Office ❑ Territories Development Department ❑ Water Supplies Department
Secretary for Economic Services	❑ Agriculture & Fisheries Department ❑ Civil Aviation Department ❑ Marine Department ❑ Office of the Telecommunications Authority ❑ Post Office ❑ Royal Observatory ❑ Secretariat, Port Development Board
Secretary for the Treasury	❑ Government Land Transport Agency ❑ Government Supplies Department ❑ Government Property Agency ❑ Information Technology Services Department ❑ Inland Revenue Department ❑ Printing Department ❑ Rating & Valuation Department ❑ Treasury
Secretary for Financial Services	❑ Census & Statistics Department ❑ Companies Registry ❑ Office of the Commissioner of Insurance ❑ Official Receiver's Office
Secretary for Trade & Industry	❑ Customs & Excise Department ❑ Industry Department ❑ Intellectual Property Department ❑ Overseas Offices ❑ Trade Department ❑ Travel Agents Registry
Chief Executive, Hong Kong Monetary Authority	

make all important appointments and to create regulations to give effect to the ordinance (s 59). Since the insurance industry launched investment-linked products, another government agency, the Security & Future Commission (SFC), has also had some influence on the operations of the insurance industry.

Insurance Supervisory Philosophy

Hong Kong's insurance supervisory philosophy generally subscribes to the operation of open market forces. A distinguishing feature of the industry is that it does not require prior government approval to launch a product; no prior approval of premium rates is required. Attempts have been made from time to time to avoid over-regulation and to encourage open market competition. Indeed, the publicized philosophy of the Insurance Commissioner are: a "friendly" regulatory body that consults closely with the industry, an open and transparent working procedure, and a will to keep abreast of international standards for the promotion professionalism and the provision of a level playing field for market players.[2]

The main provisions of the 1983 ordinance authorizes "fit and proper" persons to offer insurance to the public when certain capital and solvency requirements are met. Insurers are also required to submit financial information which can be subjected to audit by the insurance commission. In some situations, the insurance commission does have the power of intervention. The Insurance Authority announces the frequency of its own instances of intervention every year in its annual report. The degree of intervention does not seem particularly high.

In the last few years, regulations governing the insurance industry have appeared to be on the increase. Additional ordinances have been introduced to strengthen the capital and the solvency margins. There are now separate solvency margins for general and long-term business. Regulations dealing with intermediaries have been "delegated" (in a certain sense) to industry self-regulating bodies. Nevertheless, the Insurance Authority has the power to direct an insurer to de-register an appointed insurance agent. It can also withdraw the authorization of an insurance broker. With regard to investment, a new law introduced in 1994 stipulated the maintenance of local assets. This law requires all general insurers, other than professional reinsurers, to maintain assets in Hong Kong of not less than 80% of net liabilities plus a "relevant" margin attributable to Hong Kong insurance business.[3]

To a great extent, the supervisory role of Hong Kong insurance rests on the self-regulating bodies. A rough count taken in a study conducted by Yip in 1994 listed twenty such bodies, not counting the Commissioner of Insurance.[4] With the emergence of the Consumer Council and the general idea of consumerism, the insurance industry may be more heavily regulated in the future according to the preferences of these self-regulating and consumer bodies. Yet, considering the industry's fundamental free market philosophy, the government and the self-regulatory bodies will have to maintain a balance between professional rules and market efficiency.

Regulatory Trends and the Political Economy of Regulation

Whenever regulation of an industry is at issue, the question arises as to how to achieve a balance between the free market principle and the professionalism that the industry requires. The former advocates minimum intervention, while the latter invites regulations, whether government or self imposed. Often, regulations in the form of ethical codes governing industry activities are necessary, as business transactions in many forms of markets must embody trust. However, an overemphasis on ethical rules can sometimes be used as a barrier to entry or as a means to enforce a cartel. When rules adopted result in anti-competitive behaviour that reduces overall market efficiency, the industry can be said to be over-regulated.

Personal interviews conducted with industry people during the course of this study did not suggest that the industry is presently over-regulated. It is interesting to note that some recent ordinances were introduced *not directly* in response to existing problems (to the extent that the public knows about them), but because of a need to "upgrade the international standard of regulation".[5] Insurers coming from heavily regulated parent countries will find the Hong Kong environment incredibly liberating. They will certainly be able to live with a slightly higher level of regulation; indeed, some believe that a little more regulation would benefit the industry.[6]

The two dangers of a slow drift towards more regulation should be restated here. (1) If the industry can attribute its past success to minimal regulation, increased regulation will decrease its competitiveness and its comparative advantages. (2) Regulation invites interest group politics, and the insurance industry will not be an exception. Theoretically at least, the problem is likely to be compounded if supervision of the industry is to acquire its autonomy while simultaneously subjected to consumerism and democratization. Hypothetically speaking, suppose that in the future the insurance industry is to be supervised by the Insurance Advisory Board. The resulting regulations are likely to be drastically different from those that would be issued if the industry were directly controlled by the governor (the future SAR Chief) or his Financial Secretary.

The question of whether or not the Insurance Authority will be able to acquire autonomy from the existing regulatory framework will demand increasing attention beyond 1997. First of all, it is not necessarily advisable for the Insurance Authority to be shielded entirely from the supervision of the Hong Kong Monetary Authority. As the argument in this and the next chapter will illustrate, there are industry trends that may call for some coordinated supervision between the banking and the insurance sectors. Likewise, agencies such as the Security and Future Commission and the Mandatory Provident Fund Office may play an increasingly large role in the supervision of the insurance industry, especially if the industry is to shift its future emphasis increasingly towards investment and long-term retirement products.

The reality of Hong Kong's integration with China also suggests the possibility that the Insurance Authority in Hong Kong be subjected to the insurance supervision of Mainland China. In principle, the Basic Law of Hong Kong should prevent this from happening. However, if the industry voluntarily accepts this kind of supervision, it is difficult to see why the Basic Law would stand in the way. Speaking realistically, China's regulatory body is also emerging, and integrating Hong Kong's and China's insurance authorities could be highly beneficial, but it could be or extremely costly. Such a move could potentially be beneficial in the sense that the Insurance Authority might be able to use the opportunity to establish Hong Kong's role in assisting Mainland China to develop its insurance industry. The move could also be very costly, however, in the sense that insurance supervision in Hong Kong may be dragged down by China's massive system.

Still another possibility is that the Insurance Authority be subjected to the supervision of a neutral body, with participation from the Mainland and possibly from the Taiwan Insurance Authority. Academic interaction between the three entities already exists. As the Commissioner of Insurance suggested in one of such recent seminars, "a closer co-operation among the 'Three Regions' in promoting the development of the study of insurance, developing new insurance products to meet the needs of the market, and expanding insurance and reinsurance business in the Asia-Pacific region will bring about an enhanced underwriting capacity . . .".[7] The role of the "Three Regions" organization could potentially be expanded to include policy and regulation matters. In order for this to happen, of course, the insurance authorities in each of the three regions would have to implicitly or explicitly acknowledge the legitimacy of such a body, which they have not yet done.

Specific Regulatory Issues in Hong Kong

The issues relevant to the insurance industry in Hong Kong are driven by the general discussion that is currently taking place in the territory.[8] The list here is obviously far from exhaustive, the main issues being related to the market structure, commission rates, and the intermediaries.

Table 4.1
Number of Financial Institutions in Hong Kong

	Types	End of 1969	End of 1992
I.	Licensed banks	73	161
	a. domestic	20	15
	b. foreign	53	146
	c. total no.of branches	362	1,409
II.	Representative banks	21	148
III.	Restricted license banks	0	55
	a. domestic	0	3
	b. foreign	0	52
IV.	Deposit-taking companies	0	146
	a. domestic	0	50
	b. foreign	0	96
V.	Insurance companies	214	237**
	a. incorporated in Hong Kong	58*	110**
	b. incorporated overseas	156**	127**
VI.	Unit trusts and mutual funds	n.a.	856
	a. incorporated in Hong Kong	n.a.	101
	b. incorporated overseas	n.a.	755

Source: Office of the Commissioner of Banking; Registrar-General's Department; and Securities and Futures Commission, from Jao, Y.C., "The Development of Hong Kong's Financial Sector 1967–92".

Note: * as of March 1971
** as of March 1992

Market Structure and Performance

It is much easier to obtain an insurance license in Hong Kong than it is to obtain a banking license. Table 4.1 gives the number of financial institutions in Hong Kong. In terms of either the gross output or the value added, the insurance industry occupies only 8% to 12% of the financial sector (based on Table 3.1 in Chapter 3). But in terms of the number of firms in existence, insurance companies are comparable to banks and deposit-taking companies. The Hong Kong Government's authorization of banks and insurance companies might reflect a difference in the two industries' approaches to the problems of moral hazard and adverse selection.

The banking industry has more often turned to the government to handle these problems, whereas in the case of insurance, which requires less capital, the industry has relied more heavily on the free market principle. This may be the reason that some people have asked whether there are too many insurance companies in Hong Kong.

In the preceding chapter, we went over the number of companies authorized to do business in different areas of insurance in Hong Kong (see Table 3.12). The number of general insurance companies ranges from the lowest in the business (86 aircraft insurance companies) to the highest (166 accident insurance companies). The more common types of insurance, such as motor vehicle liability insurance, general liability insurance, and damage to property insurance (each of which has more than 20% of the total gross premium of the insurance business in general) have 115, 149, and 156 authorizations, respectively.

Information from the Census and Statistics Department of the Hong Kong has been used to double check the data provided by the Insurance Authority. The distribution given in Table 3.13 of Chapter 3 indicates that there were 172 insurance establishments in Hong Kong in 1993. Comparing that number with that of the total of 229 authorized insurers operating in that year unveils a large discrepancy between the two figures. This discrepancy may be a result of: (1) Registered insurers relying entirely on independent agents and brokers to sell insurance for them, in which case maintaining a local office has not been necessary; (2) A parent company acting as a holding company of several subsidiaries. While all entities are registered with the Insurance Authority, only the subsidiaries and not the holding company conduct business transactions; (3) A registered insurer being dormant and non-operating.

The characteristics of the small firms in the industry in 1993 are revealing. For general insurers, twenty-one establishments have an annual income and receipts of less than HK$5 million. Five of these twenty-one have no reported employees or persons engaged. The remaining establishments reported two to five employees. Among life insurers, twelve have an income and receipts of less than HK$5 million and employed an average of 0.6 to 1.4 people per firm.

Based on estimated profitability, certain lines of business were not that attractive, either. The underwriting margin of general liability has been negative for four consecutive years since 1991. Motor vehicle's underwriting margins were negative in 1991 and 1992 but has now turned positive. The overall underwriting margin for general insurance in 1994 was 13.4%.[9]

In spite of some evidence of capacity redundancy, the large number of firms may be the result of a low capital margin requirement rather than of a structural-conduct issue typically discussed in the field of industrial organization in economics. Insurers may want to "get a foot in the door", if it is not too expensive to do so.[10] A large number of firms, even though some may be dormant, is not sufficient information to demonstrate that there is an oversupply of firms. The essence of a competitive market is to allow free entry and exit. Firms enter an industry for many reasons; some may be directly related to profit in the short-term sense of the word, and some may not. For a mature market such as Hong Kong's, to second guess the reason for which a firm enters a market is purely a guess. It cannot, or should not, be a basis for regulation.[11]

One aspect of the conduct-structural issue of the insurance industry of Hong Kong is worth contemplating, however. The intertemporal dynamics of an insurer under a free competitive environment may want to lower the premium rate and increase the commission rate to attract business (see Chapter 2). This will be particularly true if the funds are to be fully insured by the government (similar to the FDIC issue in the case of American banking). For a moderate penetration rate of 40% in the life insurance business, this will pose no visible problem, as a firm's premiums are likely to accumulate at a faster rate than the rate of claims it has to pay out. So long as investment income is normal and claims in a particular year are not unusually large, a firm can "gamble" on offering a low premium rate and a high commission rate. The same cannot be said for a more mature market. If an industry's growth rate is slowing down in terms of premiums received in a given year, and if the size of claims that have to be paid out is climbing, the probability of firms falling below the solvency margin will be higher. Under those circumstances, the solvency margin should be adjusted accordingly. In any case, no sensible economic regulation can safeguard completely against failing firms.

The question of whether there may be too many firms should therefore be approached from a conduct angle rather than from a structural angle. Regulating the number of firms purely for the sake of having fewer of them makes no economic or practical sense. It is nevertheless worthwhile to look into the conduct of the companies and to examine whether the above conjecture is in fact true. If it is, to what extent is it caused by the guaranty fund, that is, the insurance fund?

Commission Rates Regulation

The issue to be discussed here is related to the point made above. In a free, competitive market, commission rates would not be regulated. However, the converse is not true. A regulated rate does not imply a lack of competition. While "price-fixing" of various types can restrict the actions of individual sellers of services through an agreement on rates, there can be non-price competition. The theoretical model describing such a view is mentioned in the theoretical section of this study (Chapter 2). In the U.S. real estate industry, for example, the commission rate is set at a uniform 6%. This rate is not literally fixed in that when economic conditions change drastically, the rate is expected to change also. In the American legal profession, rates are sometimes fixed as well. Commission rate fixing is therefore not necessarily incompatible with free competition. Both industries are characterized by a very large number of sellers, so it is quite inconceivable that the reason behind the rate-fixing is collusion for the purpose of creating a monopoly rent.

In Hong Kong, the insurance industry is co-ordinated by a complicated web of commission relationships between brokers and

Figure 4.2
Commission Relationship between Brokers and Agents, between Insurers and Reinsurers

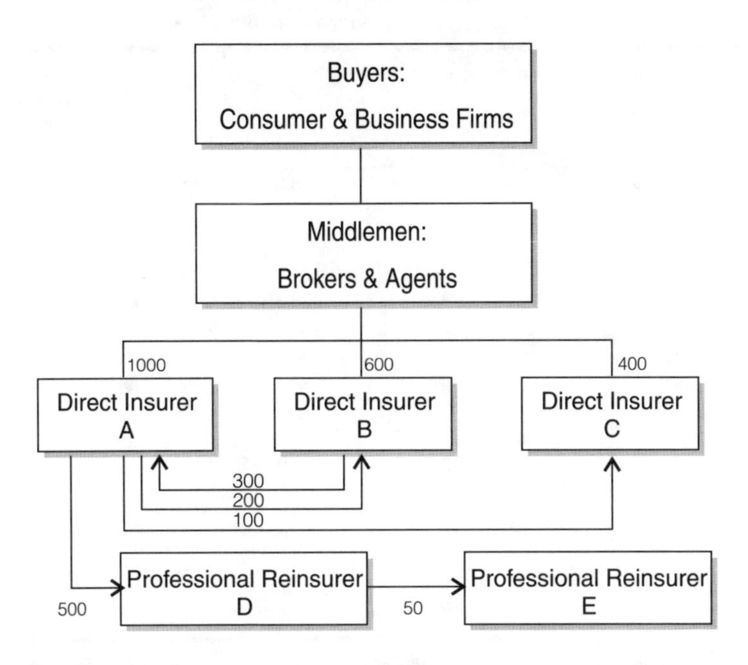

agents, as well as between insurers and reinsurers. Figure 4.2 captures the essence of these relationships. As an example, suppose someone (through a broker or agent middleman) bought $1,000 worth of insurance from Direct Insurer A, $600 from Direct Insurer B, and $400 from Direct Insurer C. All insurers can cede a portion of their business to another insurer or to a professional reinsurer D. A cedes $200 to B, $100 to C, and $500 to the professional insurer D. B cedes half of his $600 worth of business to A, and C does not cede any portion of his business to anyone. A in this case must pay commission on the direct business of $1000, but he receives commission on the $800 ceded to B, C, and D. The commission rates A pays the middlemen and the commission rates B, C, and D each separately pays A are all different. The relationships between A, B, C, and D may be co-ordinated by a set of annual treaties, in

Table 4.2
General Insurance Business Commission Ratio

(A) Direct & Reinsurance Inward Business

Class of Business	Commission Payable Ratio				Commission Receivable Ratio			
	1991 (%)	1992 (%)	1993 (%)	1994 (%)	1991 (%)	1992 (%)	1993 (%)	1994 (%)
Accident & Health	19.4	19.0	18.0	18.8	18.8	32.2	30.0	28.4
Motor Vehicle	30.7	30.0	19.5	19.7	25.9	29.6	21.9	20.5
Aircraft	20.5	6.9	12.0	11.9	–	60.7	33.3	10.9
Ships	12.0	12.2	11.5	11.6	17.7	18.3	17.3	15.0
Goods In Transit	23.1	22.9	23.4	23.3	26.1	25.7	28.3	28.0
Property Damage	36.8	36.3	38.0	36.6	42.9	43.3	42.7	38.7
General Liability	30.0	30.7	28.2	19.0	23.2	22.2	20.8	18.2
Pecuniary Loss	24.6	18.9	19.5	16.6	27.4	20.7	20.1	18.4
Non-Proportional Treaty	9.0	8.7	7.9	4.8	3.7	2.4	2.1	2.2
Proportional Treaty	35.3	37.4	34.4	33.9	29.8	31.2	32.9	31.8
Overall	29.8	29.3	26.5	24.6	32.5	32.4	30.3	27.6

(B) Direct Business

Class of Business	Commission Payable on Ratio				Commission Receivable Ratio			
	1991 (%)	1992 (%)	1993 (%)	1994 (%)	1991 (%)	1992 (%)	1993 (%)	1994 (%)
Accident & Health	19.0	18.7	17.5	18.2	28.6	32.6	30.7	28.9
Motor Vehicle	30.9	30.4	18.8	19.2	24.8	24.8	20.5	20.1
Aircraft	–	3.2	–	4.8	–	13.8	33.3	5.0
Ships Statutory	15.0	15.3	13.9	11.7	17.2	19.1	17.4	15.8
Others	10.3	11.5	10.4	10.6	17.5	18.1	17.4	15.4
Goods In Transit	22.8	22.7	23.1	23.0	26.4	26.0	28.1	28.5
Property Damage	38.1	38.8	40.3	39.1	45.1	45.5	45.6	41.4
General Liability Statutory	32.0	32.6	29.7	18.9	23.4	21.9	20.1	17.2
Others	20.1	21.4	20.9	20.3	22.9	22.5	23.3	23.3
Pecuniary Loss	22.9	18.7	19.1	16.0	27.0	20.4	19.9	17.8
Overall	29.4	29.4	25.7	23.6	33.3	33.3	30.7	27.5

Table 4.2
General Insurance Business Commission Ratio

(C) Reinsurance Inward Business

Class of Business	Commission Payable Ratio				Commission Receivable Ratio			
	1991 (%)	1992 (%)	1993 (%)	1994 (%)	1991 (%)	1992 (%)	1993 (%)	1994 (%)
Accident & Health	28.8	23.2	25.7	27.0	19.6	18.4	20.3	21.2
Motor Vehicle	28.6	27.1	23.1	22.5	29.6	30.3	28.3	25.1
Aircraft	6.0	7.9	12.2	12.6	–	–	–	14.3
Ships	17.8	13.8	13.9	13.5	19.1	18.8	16.8	12.8
Goods In Transit	24.4	23.9	24.4	25.1	23.6	23.5	30.2	21.6
Property Damage	34.1	20.9	33.5	33.5	33.1	31.0	29.6	30.3
General Liability	26.9	25.6	23.6	18.9	22.6	25.8	21.5	18.5
Pecuniary Loss	28.7	20.1	21.7	18.9	30.7	23.7	21.4	21.6
Non-Proportional Treaty	9.0	8.7	7.9	4.8	3.7	2.4	2.1	2.2
Proportional Treaty	35.5	37.4	34.4	33.9	29.8	31.2	32.9	31.8
Overall	31.1	29.2	29.1	27.8	29.4	28.7	29.0	28.0

(D) Professional Reinsurers' Business

Class of Business	Commission Payable Ratio				Commission Receivable Ratio			
	1991 (%)	1992 (%)	1993 (%)	1994 (%)	1991 (%)	1992 (%)	1993 (%)	1994 (%)
Accident & Health	30.2	30.2	31.9	34.4	31.0	–	31.0	28.1
Motor Vehicle	28.1	24.5	16.6	24.5	–	–	–	8.8
Aircraft	4.9	8.7	12.2	12.7	–	–	–	–
Ships	20.3	21.6	21.7	20.6	19.6	21.1	16.1	20.3
Goods In Transit	25.3	24.0	23.6	26.9	21.6	15.6	17.2	20.3
Property Damage	33.1	32.3	33.7	33.3	24.1	25.5	28.5	27.1
General Liability	25.0	27.3	23.0	21.1	28.2	28.4	23.1	22.6
Pecuniary Loss	20.3	15.7	23.0	23.8	24.0	23.3	25.0	25.0
Non-Proportional Treaty	5.5	6.0	5.9	4.6	8.0	4.3	5.4	5.3
Proportional Treaty	42.1	42.1	39.0	39.1	38.4	41.5	37.5	32.7
Overall	32.7	31.6	30.3	30.8	29.8	32.5	31.1	28.5

Source: Office of the Commissioner of Insurance and the Registrar of Occupational Retirement Schemes Hong Kong, *Annual Report 1995*, p.81.

which case the ceding of premium and the calculation of commission is automatic. In other cases, the ceding process is negotiated on a case-by-case basis often involving brokers. Thus, each insurer pays as well as receives a commission. This is true for direct insurers A, B, and C, as well as for professional reinsurer D. In the latter case, $50 of the $500 received by D is ceded to E. Therefore, there is commission payable and receivable even for a reinsurer.

The aggregate commission rates for different areas in the general insurance industry of Hong Kong are given in Table 4.2 (*1995 Annual Report*, p. 17). Because of the way in which commission in the industry is organized (as was described in the previous paragraph), there are separate tabulations for commission payable and commission receivable. The commission payable ratio is defined as the commission payable as a percentage of gross premiums. The commission receivable ratio is defined as the commission receivable as a percentage of ceded premiums. The ratios can be further segregated into three categories of direct insurance, reinsurance inward business, and professional reinsurers business. For example, using the numbers in Figure 4.2, direct insurance business is $2,000 (= 1,000 + 600 + 400). Reinsurance inward business is $1,150 (= 300 + 200 + 100 + 500 + 50). Professional reinsurance business is $550 (= 500 + 50).

In 1994 property damage insurance had the highest commission rate payable in the industry (39.1% for direct business and 32.2% for reinsurance inward business). Nonproportional treaty insurance had the lowest commission rate payable (4.8% for reinsurance inward business). Several patterns were further observed: (1) The commission receivable ratio was generally higher than the commission payable ratio, reflecting a higher commission rate for reinsurance business than for direct business; (2) Different classes of business have different rates, but the rates have been declining overall since 1991; and (3) Motor vehicle insurance rates dropped most sharply in 1993, and general liability insurance rates dropped most sharply in 1994. The latter phenomenon reflected a

January 1994 agreement to restrict the commission rate for employee compensation insurance to a maximum of 15%.

Practically speaking, the reported rates are not necessarily the rates specified in actual agency contracts with agents and brokers. There are two reasons for this: (1) There can be variations in rates within a type of business; and (2) Commission can be paid to the insurer rather than to the agents (or the brokers). Nevertheless, Table 4.2 can serve as approximate estimates of the insurance commission rates in Hong Kong.

From the regulatory perspective, what is more relevant are the actual contract rates between insurers and intermediaries. For motor vehicle and employee compensation insurance, which together make up 81% of general liability insurance, the Insurance Authority has at one point suggested a 15% rate cap. This suggestion has been subsequently endorsed by most insurers in the business. The question of whether this is a government-regulated rate or an industry self-imposed rate is not a useful one to dwell upon here, except for the purpose of ideological debate. At issue is whether there is a fundamental non-cartel reason for the rate fixing and whether there will be a corresponding decrease in the service of the middlemen. In 1994 the gross premium in motor vehicle insurance declined, while in all other areas of insurance it increased. For general liability insurance, the increase was the largest, at 45.8%.

A more in-depth investigation and a continuous dialogue of the effects of the commission rate cap on motor and employee compensation insurance is probably desirable. At this point, several comments about the rate cap can be made:

(1) The Insurance Authority explains the decrease in gross premium in motor vehicle insurance in terms of a reduction in the number of newly registered motor vehicles that year.[12] However, in view of the overall increase in the number of *total* licensed vehicles, there may in fact be *more* uninsured motorists on the streets. On the other

hand, the reduction in premium would have been caused by a reduction in premium rates also. In that case, there might not be any increase; in fact, there may actually have been a decrease in the number of uninsured motorists. This is therefore an empirical question that needs to be further researched and studied.

(2) The Insurance Authority also explains the large increase in gross premium in general liability insurance in terms of a 40% increase in the employee compensation tariff rating.[13] It is not clear what this really implies about economic efficiency. At the very least, it reflects the pitfalls of using a high reported growth rate (45.8% in general liability insurance, in this case) as an indication of prosperity. In economic terms, if the increase is due to the tariff, a welfare triangle is likely to be created, and the quantity demanded for this service ought to be less, not more.

Yet, viewed from a different angle, the commission rate cap for motor vehicle and employee compensation insurance is justified, if cut-throat competition is indeed taking place. As was described earlier, an insurer can cut premium rates while raising commission rates to "gamble" for a lower claim rate. If the claim exceeds the lower expectation, the insurer can declare bankruptcy. The incentive to do this will be high if there are guaranty funds for the firms' failure. Indeed, for both motor vehicle and employee insurance compensation, there are funds that would cover claims in the case of insurers' insolvency. The extent to which the funds have been utilized is an empirical question. While desegregate data at the firm level needs to be analysed in more detail to verify this conjecture, a 1987 MBA thesis at the University of Hong Kong had provided the following description of the motor vehicle insurance industry,

> "This is the only class that tariff rates really exist so that insurers compete severely on commission rates. Furthermore, smaller insurers who want to accumulate a large fund quickly are prone to pick this class in offering cut-

price premiums because the policies are simple and it is best for direct marketing. This will confuse the product pricing of other companies."[14]

The tariff referred to is most likely a contribution to the guaranty funds operated by the Motor Insurers' Bureau.[15] Writing in 1987, two years after the fund scheme was set up, the writer could not have known that another guaranty fund for employee compensation was going to be erected in 1990.

Nowadays, aside from a moral hazard factor generated by the guaranty funds, an evaluation of the overall economic efficiency of commission rate regulations in motor vehicle insurance and employee compensation insurance must take into consideration the development of direct sales. Direct sales refers to the more recent marketing techniques of using telephone, direct mail, company employees, and mass advertising to gain access to potential customers. In the areas of motor vehicle and employee compensation insurance, there may be an overall reduction in the service quality offered by agents and brokers, but if such a gap is filled by direct sales, consumers have little to lose. A related question is that of whether the commission rate cap will speed up the development of direct sales, which may occur in the area of motor vehicle insurance anyway. The increase in benefits due to an earlier introduction of direct sales would have to be subtracted from the efficiency loss in agent and broker service quality. If the former more than offsets the latter, then commission rate regulation may be efficient.

Intermediaries Regulatory Structure

In the United States, there are two main marketing systems for selling insurance: the independent agency system (sometimes called the American Agency System) and the direct writing system (sometimes called the direct selling system). The independent agent is an independent business person who owns and finances his or her agency, and who is compensated through commissions that vary depending on the type of insurance and company. An independent agent usually represents several companies. Direct writing, on the other hand, involves the sale of insurance through the mail or through exclusive agents. An exclusive agent is an employee of a specific insurance company and is only able to sell insurance issued by that company. An exclusive agent is usually compensated on a "salary plus" arrangement which consists of a basic salary plus a commission.

The agency systems of Hong Kong and the U.S. are not identical, but they are also not drastically different. It can be said that Hong Kong's agency system is going through a period of change and may be growing more similar to the U.S. system. Yet, Hong Kong's system has its own path to follow, and this path may be different from what a theoretical categorization suggests.

Traditionally, the Hong Kong agency system has followed the European system of agents and brokers.[16] In theory, insurance brokers differ from insurance agents in that the former represent insurance buyers and not insurance companies. Insurance companies are represented by agents. In this sense, brokers in Hong Kong do resemble those of the independent agency system in the U.S. Viewed from this perspective, brokers can be seen as independent agents, in the theoretical sense of the term. However, many agents in Hong Kong represent buyers also. Indeed, it is worth questioning whether the 2,134 insurance establishments listed by the Census & Statistics Department of the Hong Kong Government should be classified as brokers or as agents. Whether an establishment is a broker or an agent may depend on its customers and the policy of the insurance company it represents.

From the legal perspective, a person cannot be appointed as an insurance agent and as an authorized insurance broker at the same time. This position has its origin in the *Insurance Companies Ordinance, Amendment No. 3*, which was issued in July 1994, and it can be construed as an attempt to move the agency system in Hong Kong closer to the "buyer versus insurer" representation dichotomy, as the theoretical meanings of the terms broker and agent intend to imply. Simultaneously, however, enforcement of conduct is left to self-regulatory systems developed by agents and brokers. Through an evolutionary process about to evolve, the agency system of Hong Kong could very well become different from that which the original legislation had intended.

At present, the self-regulating system of the industry is applied to individual agents and company agents. For individual agents, the Hong Kong Federation of Insurers (a trade organization consisting of 126 general insurer members and 49 life insurer members)[17] issued a Code of Practice for Administration of Insurance Agents in 1993. The Code of Practice requires appointed agents of an insurance company to register with an Insurance Agents Registration Board (IARB). An insurance agent is prohibited from representing more than four insurers, of which not more than two can be long-term insurers. The Board has disciplinary powers against insurance agents registered with it and handles complaints involving premium misappropriation, concealment, misrepresentation, forgery, twisting of policies, service, and other matters. In 1994 there were 2,412 company agents and 17,592 individual agents in Hong Kong. Among the individuals registered, 22% were in general insurance, 25% were in life insurance, and 53% were in both. For company agents, the majority (85%), were in general insurance, only 2% were in life insurance, and 13% were in both the life and non-life insurance businesses.[18] As of March 1996, IARB has 3,449 registered company agents and 25,820 individual agents.[19]

In order to implement self regulations, brokers join professional bodies approved by the Insurance Authority. At present, brokers can join either the Professional Insurance Broker Association (PIBA) or the Hong Kong Confederation of Insurance Brokers (CIB). The former was established in 1987, and the latter was set up in 1993. While the criteria and the emphases of the two associations may be different, the Broker Association's membership requirements are not that different from those of the Insurance Authority. To be an insurance broker in Hong Kong, a person or company must have a minimum capital and net asset value of not less than HK$100,000, must satisfy some minimum education and experience requirements, must carry sufficient professional indemnity insurance, and must have sets of the proper books for both himself and his clients. The *1993 Manpower Survey* covered 38 "major" insurance brokers. But as of July 1994 the CIB had 68 members, while the PIBA had 50.[20] In May 1996 the official count of CIB members was 191, while that of the PIBA was 114. In addition, two brokers had registered directly via the Commissioner of Insurance.

Government regulation of intermediaries and self-regulating bodies in Hong Kong is an interdependent dynamic process which is expected to go through some evolutionary changes. At this point, the emphasis has been on the rights and the protection of the consumer, more than on anything else. An explicit discussion of promotional efforts and property rights to client lists (Chapter 2) is nowhere to be found in the regulations. This, however, does not imply that the industry will not serendipitously begin moving in that direction in the future. For example, the CIB, although it is a relatively new organization, has attempted to differentiate itself from the PIBA. Aside from requiring its members to meet a set of standards of prudence, the CIB's regulations "specify that a member of the Confederation must not be dependent on any particular insurance company in transacting normal insurance business. Its name must not be such as likely to deceive . . .".[21] In addition, government or self-imposed regulation can change the dynamics of interactions. For example, a cap on the rate of commission, especially for general insurance, is expected to change the way in which insurers and brokers will do business. Ultimately, the industry structure is expected to be determined not only by regulation and by the preferences of insurers and intermediaries, but by technology and the preferences of the final consumer, as well.

Investment strategies

Studies of the insurance industry of Hong Kong performed by the Hongkong Bank have provided the main source of information on the investment strategies of insurance companies in Hong Kong. Table 3.14 in Chapter 3 documents the growth of the financial versus the fixed assets of the industry from 1986 to 1992 for 112 general insurers and 49 life insurers. Financial assets occupied more than 98% of the total assets of general insurers as well as of life insurers. In 1992 the value of life insurers' total assets amounted to about three times that of general insurers' total assets. Table 3.15 provides a breakdown of the assets into various categories, with stocks, shares, and bonds occupying the largest share (40%) in 1992. A prominent feature of the asset portfolio of insurance companies is the relatively high percentage of deposits and cash balances. They were at 23.3% in 1992, and have remained at above 19% since 1984. Economists sometimes see this portfolio structure as conducive to the misappropriation of funds, and they may actually imply that few insurance companies will go public, even if they are given the opportunity to do so. Practitioners, on the other hand, see this portfolio structure as providing a liquidity cushion to meet sudden increases in claims.

Perhaps the most controversial item affecting the investments of general insurers in Hong Kong is the recently enacted ordinance which requires that 80% of a certain portion of general insurers' liabilities plus the solvency margin be maintained in the form of local assets (Part IVA of the *Insurance Company Ordinance*, s.25A(3)). The reason given for the issuance of this ordinance is that it increases the security of the system. It has been suggested that although an insurer may have adequate reserves to meet future claims or a sudden increase in claims, he may not be able to "actually meet the claims" if most of his assets are located outside Hong Kong. The 80% rule on the maintenance of local asset was created in the hope of increasing stability in this regard by making sure insurers doing local business have easy access to these assets if in fact the situation calls for them.

This argument needs to be examined in more detail. In the first place, while it is true that assets outside Hong Kong could be unilaterally withheld by the outside jurisdictions and in that sense are "not secure," there could be financial risks associated with holding assets in Hong Kong, as well. In principle, political and financial risks are interchangeable; both could affect the value of an asset. Political confiscation assumes a more drastic change in the value of an asset from the market value to zero.[22] However, market risks can be severe, also. Aside from daily fluctuations, a single trader's action on the derivative market can bankrupt an institution. The issue therefore may have more to do with the estimation of risks rather than with the locality of an asset.

If security is the motivation behind the Ordinance, it is not clear that the 80% local asset maintenance rule can serve the objective well. A doomsday scenario in which a fall in property value triggers a fall in stock prices and mortgage bond values can be easily simulated. The domino effect would affect the insurance industry so drastically that not even an 80% constraint could save it. Indeed, if such a situation is more likely to be triggered from within rather than from outside Hong Kong, the 80% rule will increase rather than decrease risks.

The Insurance Authority should be concerned about the liquidity and not the locality of the investment portfolio. As was pointed out in previous paragraphs, Hong Kong insurance companies already appear to be keeping a very high deposit and cash balance (23.3% in 1992). For the purpose of managing economic or political risks, presumably all that should be required is an additional risk-based adjustment in the calculation of reserves. While this would raise the cost of accounting, it would reduce the chance of having to make a second-best investment.

It is actually not clear that the 80% rule is binding. Appendix C provides a definition, taken from Eighth Schedule of the *Hong Kong Insurance Companies Ordinance*, of what the Insurance Authority would consider to be "local assets". S25C(1) also makes provisions for the use of letters of credit or other commitments from a bank as substitutes for the maintenance of local assets.

> "An insurer may, instead of maintaining assets in Hong Kong as required by this Part, substitute, in whole or in part, a letter of credit or other commitment from a bank, as defined in the Banking Ordinance (Cap.155), in favor of the Insurance Authority, but the terms and conditions at-

tached to such a letter of credit of other commitment are subject to the approval of the Insurance Authority."

The extent to which this provision has been utilized is not yet known. If it has not been extensively utilized, the 80% rule may have been non-binding and thus a moot issue. On the other hand, if it has been used extensively, it is possible that (1) insurers have viewed a rearrangement of their asset portfolio as too costly and prefer banks to provide support of the necessary liquidity, even though it will probably involve additional fees; or (2) the alleged outside locality risk will be shifted to the banks, and the higher risks imposed on the latter would have to be addressed by the Banking Authority. If it is desirable to examine how the Hong Kong insurance sector can stimulate the economy, more investigative research work into this issue may be called for.

Summary

Proper weights have to be assigned to the objectives of the free market principle, professionalism, and security in the years to come. It does not seem possible to discuss this issue as a purely "within the industry" matter. Broadly speaking, the jurisdiction governing the Insurance Authority of post-1997 Hong Kong is an issue that requires thoughtful consideration. The political economy of the industry is complicated, and whatever the future regulatory framework will emerge, it will shape the character of the industry and significantly affect the enforcement of future regulations. At a more micro-management level, the Insurance Authority may want to avoid regulation for the mere sake of keeping up with international standards. While changes are bound to occur in response to a new economic environment, new technology, new problems and so on, the maintenance of the free market principle should be afforded substantial weight in all new regulatory considerations.

Notes

1. Tashjian and Cooray (1995), Chapter 7, p. 181.
2. Speech given by the Insurance Commissioner, 25 March 1996.
3. Part IVA of the *Insurance Company Ordinance*. A summary statement of this ordinance was provided in the *Insurance Supervisory System in Hong Kong*, a paper prepared by the Insurance Authority, April 1996. The definition of "relevant" margin can be found in Part IVA of the Ordinance, S.25A.
4. pp. 38–39.
5. This is more of a general impression and is not an official statement that is clearly stated in public records. Commissioner's Annual Report, 1994, however, declared that the Commissioner will "continue to review and update the Insurance Companies Ordinance to bring them in line with internal as well as internal developments."
6. The 1983 ordinance has been credited with providing a stabilizing factor for the industry which was experiencing several failures of motor vehicle insurers.
7. Opening remarks by the Commissioner of Insurance at the Insurance Seminar organized by the Hong Kong Federation of Insurers, 24 and 25 April 1996
8. Some of the issues can be found in *The Services Sector Support and Promotion, The 1996–97 Budget Addendum* provided by the Financial Secretary of the Hong Kong Government. See in particular the section on *Insurance Services* by the Secretary for Financial Services, March 1996. The issues discussed there will be discussed here in the next chapter.
9. Underwriting margin is defined as underwriting profit (loss) as a percentage of earned premiums. Earned premium is gross premium minus reinsured amount minus an amount set aside for technical reserve called "unearned premium". It is an *underestimation* of real economic profit, because one would expect interest to be earned on technical reserve.
10. Indeed, early in 1995, some analysts believed that a licensed insurer in Hong Kong could be granted to operate throughout China after 1997, even though he would still have to go through a review process. See *Asia & Pacific Insurance Newsletter, Issue No. 20, January 1995.*
11. This does not imply that the same criteria should apply to an emerging market such as Mainland China. There, the question is not so much on how to establish the criteria for entry. There is obviously a need for such criteria in an emerging market, but the question has more to do with

regulatory transparency. (See Chapter 2 for an elaboration of the problems regulators face.)

12. *Annual Report,* 1995, p. 15.

13. ibid.

14. Kwong (1987), p. 60.

15. The Motor Insurers' Bureau currently collects a levy close to HK$100 million a year. In 1994 a total of 38 First Fund claims amounting to HK$20 million were submitted. In 1995 a total of 43 claims with reserves of HK$14 million were received. It is worth noting that in 1990 and 1991 three motor insurance companies were insolvent. A total of 149 claims were involved, and claims reserves totaled over HK$113 million. As of April 1996 there are still 35 claims outstanding with reserves of HK$33 million. Speech given by Mr. Fred Dougherty, Deputy Chairman, Motor Insurers' Bureau, 25 April 1996.

16. Yip (1994) p. 35. A government representative has also mentioned the introduction of management guidelines from Europe, Sing Tao Daily, 27 April 1996.

17. *Annual Report*, The Hong Kong Federation of Insurers, 1994–1995.

18. Yip (1994), p. 36.

19. "Insurance Agents Registration Board," speech given by Mr. Dennis Pedini, member of IARB, 25 April 1996.

20. Yip (1994), p. 61.

21. Tashjian and Cooray (1995), p. 193. The point has also been emphasized in the author's interview with the President of CIB, Mr. Michael Haynes.

22. To be precise, even confiscated assets might not have a zero value. It depends on the legal procedures for getting the assets back in the jurisdiction.

CHAPTER 5

Building a Competitive Edge: Institutional Development

Hong Kong can more effectively utilize its resources in improving the competitive advantages in the field of insurance. A year before the historical transition of 1997 was to take place, the Deputy Chairman of the Hong Kong Federation of Insurers, Mr. Steven Lau, attributed the past success of the industry to a good mix of the government, businessmen, and the workforce:

> "[The] success [of Hong Kong] has been built on the basis of a stable economy, laissez-faire government policy, low tax, a sound and respected legal system, sophisticated infrastructure, excellent communications, shrewd entrepreneurship and an industrious work force."[1]

The question of competitive advantages extends this position to see how success can be maintained in the future. This chapter is concerned with institutional development for creating a competitive edge.

The issue can also be phrased in terms of strategic alliances which are some form of institutional development. As a start, we shall describe a prominent feature of the existing institutional alliance in Hong Kong, one between banks and insurance companies. Other strategic alliance possibilities exist from the points of view of industrial co-operation; geographical localities; and political, investment, and tax innovations. These possibilities will be discussed in the latter part of this chapter.

Insurance Companies and Banks

Insurance companies are financial institutions that are fundamentally similar to other financial institutions. They assemble funds in the form of premiums and disburse claims from their reserves when "accidental" events trigger losses. The insurance principle operates on the assumption that customers will not all appear on the same day to make claims, especially immediately after their policies are purchased. Similarly, banks do not expect their customers to withdraw all the money from their accounts immediately after the accounts are opened. Insurance companies earn the difference between the amounts of the premiums received and the amount of the anticipated claims. They use these earnings for various investments, thereby earning an investment income. In short, insurance companies provide two types of services, loss protection and investment management.

Insurance companies and banks differ in many ways, however. First and most obviously, they differ in their physical appearances. The contractual relationships of each of the two types of institutions with their customers are also different. Moral hazard and adverse selection problems are much more severe for an insurance contract than they are for a regular bank deposit or loan contract. Banks accept customers from all income levels and social strata. One's habits, the way in which one earns a living, and one's spending and saving patterns are all irrelevant to a bank. In contrast, insurance companies are relatively focused on certain targeted markets. As was pointed out in Chapter 2, screening and signalling have to be used to reduce adverse selection. Therefore, restrictive provisions are more often adopted by insurance contracts than by bank contracts to reduce moral hazard and adverse selection.

There is a second way in which banks and insurance companies can differ. Accident and death rates for the population as a whole are predictable, usually by statisticians and actuaries, with a high degree of accuracy. Insurance companies can thus have better control of their payouts to policyholders, and consequently of their future liabilities. For banks, the preference for cash and demand deposits in a particular bank fluctuates more in terms of the amount withdrawn and the frequency of withdrawals, and thus it is more difficult to estimate in terms of the flow of funds in and out of an institution.

The third difference between banks and insurance companies is that banks are more likely to be affected by macroeconomic factors such as central bank lending policies, interest rates, business cycles, investment and stock market sentiments. The assets of banks might also be more closely tied with assets in a particular area, such as mortgage contracts. Thus, regional fluctuation of the economy will have a large impact on the banking industries that tend to do only local business. For both of these reasons, life insurance companies are less likely to experience widespread failures of the type the commercial banks in the U.S. have experienced.

The higher risk of operating banks as compared to insurance companies may imply that banks need to rely to some extent on a strategic alliance with insurance companies in order to solve short-term liquidity problems. Insurance companies, similarly, may wish to seek strategic alliances with banks, because the two institutions can share marketing facilities and investment expertise. Insurance companies that are against this alliance incentive sometimes argue that the instability of the banking industry, e.g., the possibility of a bank run, is too high a price to pay for the benefits that would arise from merging the two types of business. They argue that customer confidence in their industry should be of the highest priority when they are considering such a move.[2] However, if the insurance companies' technical reserves are correctly calculated and well enforced, the increased risk of including banking assets in an insurance company's assets should be treated, at least theoretically, as any other risky investment that an insurance company might want to undertake. Thus, including the banking asset into an insurance company's investment portfolio need not be a major concern.

In practice, an insurance company may have concentrated too much on a particular type of asset in its portfolio choice. A large proportion of assets vested in a particular institution will transport the risk of that institution to the net worth of the insurance company, which should not be borne by the company's regular policyholders. These are risks that might not be easily diversified away. The recent and drastic change in the financial health of insurance companies resulting from the long real estate slump in Japan is an example of such a situation. In this respect, the potential risk of extensive linkage of real estate, banks, and the insurance industry in Hong Kong should not be overlooked at all.

Overall, the reasons for banks and insurance companies to form alliances seem compelling, and the industry has certainly been moving in that direction. Identifying the fact that there is much to gain by forming alliances does not, however, necessarily imply that alliances will be formed. In the U.S., whether it is the bank or the insurance company that makes the first move towards forming an alliance has been of some significance. As Santomero (1993, p.18) observed, the insurance industry in the U.S. has increasingly viewed itself as part of the financial service industry and includes such financial market products as securities and commercial and mortgage banking, among others. The industry considers this evolution to be "a natural outgrowth of its comparative advantages which includes asset management skills, substantial financial resources, and a large customer base." Understandably, it sees the bank's move into the insurance industry as a threat to its long-term strategy. Creating an alliance between banks and insurance companies, therefore, has not been a smooth process in the United States. Hong Kong has never been in a parallel situation, probably because of the absence of the equivalent of the Glass-Steagall Act in the territory.[3] Also, there is no government deposit insurance in Hong Kong, and thus there is no room for the "source of strength" argument to surface here, as it has in the U.S.[4] Subjected to the risk factor mentioned in the last paragraph, this regulatory environment provides an advantage that alliances between banking and insurance in Hong Kong can enjoy, but that U.S. institutions cannot.

Another issue that will greatly influence the forming of strategic alliance between banks and insurance in the future is that of bancassurance, which allow retail bank customers to buy insurance while they are in the bank The power of bancassurance is that by utilizing technologies, the alliance will be able to serve all rather than just some of its customers' needs. It also provides a method for the integration of financial services into a single interface with the customer. The concept is more popular in Europe than it is in Asia,[5] but considering the trend in Asia, factors caused by the economies of scale may eventually have an impact in this area, also.

Information on the alliance between banks and insurance is not available from the Insurance Authority of Hong Kong. The only public information that can be found on the subject is in a 1990 University of Hong Kong MBA thesis. Table 5.1 gives a snapshot of the description of bank-insurance alliances in 1990. Clearly, banks' involvement with insurance was extensive at that time, and there is no reason to believe that it has lessened since then.[6] While documenting the current state of affairs between the two industries would be a valuable academic exercise, the research currently being conducted focuses more on *why and how* than on *who owns what.*

Insurance and Other Areas

Examples of insurance linkages with other businesses are abundant. Travel agencies with travel insurance, shipping companies with goods-in-transit insurance, marine insurance with seaports, health insurance with hospitals, fire insurance with construction and real estate companies — the possibilities for alliances stretch far. Certainly, risk diversification is still an important motivation for seeking an alliance, but one of the main themes pointed out in this study is that contractual consideration in terms of *management* and the *institutional features* should also be examined when such alliances are to be formed. In the rest of this chapter, we will discuss how alliances of different emphases can be considered. Issues having to do with localities, types of insurance, and the competitive position in relation to retirement fund management are examined. The discussion of these questions will be partly descriptive and partly suggestive.

Table 5.1
Strategic Alliance of Banks and Insurance Companies of Hong Kong in 1990

Name of Banking Group	Major Insurers
The Hongkong & Shanghai Bank	Carlingford
Bank of China Group	Ming An, China & Tai Ping
Hang Seng Bank	Associated Bankers & Union Ins.
Standard Chartered	AIU & Cigna
Bank of East Asia	AIU, Lombard & Ming An
Dao Heng Bank Group	Dao Heng Insurance
Overseas Trust Bank	OTB Assurance
Shanghai Commercial Bank	Paofoong Insurance
Bank of Credit & Commerce	Commercial Union
Dah Sing Bank	Tugu
Citi-Bank	Eagle Star
Liu Chong Hing	Liu Chong Hing Insurance
Kwong On Bank	Sumitomo Insurance
Ka Wah Bank	Ka Wah Amev Insurance
First Pacific Bank	Far East Insurance

Source: Based on Table 50 in Yeung (1990 MBA thesis, The University of Hong Kong).

The China Factor

The potential of the China market exists not only because of the size of China's population, but also because of a need arising as a result of the economic reforms of the country. In recent years, responsibilities vested in SOE (state-owned enterprises) have been gradually delegated to separate and independent units of operation; to use western terminology, there has been a movement towards marketization and privatization. China's new socioeconomic structure is bound to create a large demand for many different types of insurance.[7]

China's insurance market is many times larger than Hong Kong's. Informal sources reported that China's insurance industry's total gross premium in 1995 was 8 billion yuan (another report estimated it at 48.2 billion yuan),[8] but the "official" figure was as high as 61 billion yuan.[9] In Guangzhou alone, there were more than 3 million life policyholders and 1.6 million family property policyholders near the end of 1995.[10] An insurance company in Hong Kong estimated that there are 25 million people in China who can afford life insurance coverage, based on an annual premium of 750 yuan (about US$90) for a monthly income of 1,200 yuan.[11]

In 1995 China had only twenty domestic insurance firms serving 1.2 billion people, as compared with 4800 such companies in the U.S. and 800 in Britain. The potential for expansion of the insurance industry in China is huge. A current estimate of the penetration rate is that it stands at less than 10%.[12] According to a Swiss report, life insurance premiums in China stand at 0.3% of the GNP, as compared with 1.22% in India and 9.94% in Japan.[13] A joint survey of 1,000 Shanghai residents conducted by The Shanghai University of Finance and Economics and the U.S.-based Watson Wyatt Worldwide in August 1995 also revealed that only 6% of those interviewed had purchased life insurance in the past three years. The study predicted that medical and retirement policies will emerge as two of the fastest-growing products in China.[14]

Also, based on a World Bank forecast, the potential capacity of the Chinese insurance market has been estimated at 250 billion yuan, with a continuous annual growth rate of 10%.[15] In such a huge market, independent entries as well as strategic alliances are necessary in order to explore all aspects of business development. Yet, foreign entries into the China market can be very difficult.[16] As of 1996 there were only four foreign entries in the country, and for those entered, licenses granted were for specific areas only. The four foreign insurance companies in China were American International Assurance Company Ltd., Tokyo Marine and Fire Insurance Company Ltd., Sedgewick of Britain, and Ming An Insurance Company of Hong Kong. The length of the queue waiting for licenses was long. Seventy-five foreign insurance companies and brokerage firms from thirteen countries have set up over 100 representative offices in Beijing and other Chinese cities.[17]

A popular method of seeking entry into the Chinese insurance market these days is via strategic alliances with existing insurance companies in China. There are many strategic partners to choose from in China. The most obvious one is PICC, the People's Insurance Company of China, which was the insurance monopoly in China until 1988.[18] As of 1996, it still maintained an 84% market share. The rest of the market was handled by twenty-four other domestic companies, of which only two operated at a national level.

Using market share as a policy guideline by which to seek strategic alliance can be misleading, however. The aggregate statistics do not give an accurate picture, because the strength of a company can vary across different localities. Each region and each metropolitan area can have a different leader. Aside from PICC, the two national companies, the China Pacific Insurance Company Ltd. and Ping An Insurance Company of China, have had varying degrees of success in different metropolitan areas. On 1 January 1996, the People's Bank of China also approved three more national companies with Chinese capital to proceed with preparatory work. They were Xinhua Life Assurance Company, Taikang Life Assurance Company, and Huatai Insurance Company.

Hong Kong insurance companies have been competing intensely for strategic alliance with these national companies. Newspaper articles frequently attempt to monitor the formation of alliances involving familiar names such as Aetna, Top Glory, National Mutual and Manulife. There are probably many other companies engaged in ongoing efforts to form such alliances, as well. For obvious reasons, individual companies may not want to fully disclose the nature of their co-operation and the progress of negotiations with potential partners.

The thing to note is that the competition for strategic partners in China may not be based on market share alone. Indeed, the larger and older a company is, the more complicated the organizational relationship that the partner must negotiate. In this respect, newer and smaller companies, and in particular, some regional companies, might have an advantage. Some regional companies in China of a smaller scale were the Agricultural and Husbandry Insurance company of Xinjiang Production and Construction

Corps, Tian An Insurance Company Ltd., and Dazhong Insurance Company Ltd.[19] A dozen or more regional life insurance companies also exist throughout China. Indeed, Manulife's alliance with Sinochem in the formation of Zhong Hong Life Insurance in Shanghai may be viewed as an example of this type of alliance.[20]

Alliances with banks are another factor discounting the notion that market share is of primary importance in the formation of strategic partnerships. As pointed out in previous sections, there has been a natural trend in Hong Kong towards the creation of an alliance between banks and insurance companies. The demarcation between banks and non-bank institutions in many developed countries is becoming increasingly unclear. In this respect, it can also be argued that foreign entries into the insurance market in China should not aim only at linking up with existing insurance companies in China, but with banks or with entities that have good reserves and a great deal of market exposure. Banks may wish to use foreign insurance companies as a *front* for their insurance operations. Foreign insurance companies, on the other hand, may view banks as a way to market their insurance products and to provide liquidity. Although the concept of bancassurance may be too new for China, its development could be rapid once the retail banking business has opened up.

While there is a high demand for foreign insurers to gain a foothold in China, both in terms of methods of co-operation and in terms of establishing market niches, Hong Kong's role as a bridge for this gap cannot be easily defined. Certainly, Hong Kong business people have advantages in dealing with China in terms of language, culture, geography, and perhaps also in terms of the territory's system of law and management; and in that sense Hong Kong insurers can in principle be very effective middlemen. Yet, in view of the large number of Chinese working outside Hong Kong, some of whom are directly under the head office of the parent company overseas, the human resource advantage will depend largely on the person. It has nothing to do with Hong Kong, per se.

As a location in which a regional office operates, Hong Kong will be increasingly unattractive, because of its high rent and escalating labour costs. As a world financial centre, Hong Kong has much to contribute, but marketing techniques in Hong Kong and China may be different. In this respect, it is in the area of institutional development, that is, the ability to form institutions and contracts to solve problems, that Hong Kong's comparative advantages can build around.[21] In practice, the abstract idea of "One country, Two systems" needs an industry to show its intricacies. The emerging relationship between Hong Kong, China, and Taiwan in the area of insurance will be quite revealing.[22]

Reinsurance Potential

Reinsurance refers to situations in which an insurer cedes part of the risk to another insurance company. Sometimes the reinsurer is another insurance company; sometimes it is a professional reinsurer. A measure of the extent of reinsurance activity is the retention ratio, which is the net premium divided by the gross premium. The difference between gross and net premium is the ceded amount. Hong Kong's retention ratio in 1994 for general insurance was 62.7%,[23] lower than the OECD 1993 average of 88% (see Table 3.1), and lower than that of some other Asian countries.[24] Generally speaking, there is quite a bit of reinsurance activity in Hong Kong.[25]

The fact that there is a lot of reinsurance activity in Hong Kong of course does not mean that Hong Kong can serve as a reinsurance centre. There are over 400 reinsurers in the world. Only twenty-two reinsurance companies, (eighteen of which are active), are located in Hong Kong. The distribution of reinsurers in Asia, according to a report provided by SCOR, is as follows: Singapore, twenty-eight, Hong Kong, nineteen; Japan, eighteen; Malaysia, seven; Taiwan, five; Philippines, five; Indonesia, four; S. Korea, four; Thailand, two; and China, one.[26] With an increase in the number of catastrophes (natural and man made), greater capital requirements are likely to be imposed on reinsurance companies throughout the world and in Asia Pacific in particular.[27] Only 8% of Lloyd's of London's business is in the Asia Pacific.[28] Of the business in Asia

Pacific, there is a slight geographical preference for Singapore as the location choice and for life insurance as the product choice. Mr. Wolfgang Droste of Cologne Reinsurance Company of Germany estimates the potential pool of reinsurance premium in ASEAN countries available to foreign reinsurers at about US$150 million, of which about one third is in Hong Kong and Taiwan.[29] Life reinsurers are anxious to enter the Asia market, even though at this point the stakes are still low. This is because reinsurers see an opportunity to develop a long-term relationship with direct insurers, take part in the shaping of standards, and possibly share in the business, as opposed to just receiving the premium revenue.[30] Indeed, the outlook for reinsurance in Asia is mixed. As Mr. Droste commented,

> "For reinsurance companies, the prospect of rapid economic growth does not automatically translate into fast-growing reinsurance premium volume. As direct writers grow and gain in underwriting expertise, they will inevitably increase in their retentions, especially in life insurance. In addition, in some emerging markets the bulk of the business will have low sums insured, well within the direct writer's retention."

From the point of view of economic theory, reinsurers are the "wholesalers" of insurance; they are the ultimate bearers of risk. To ask whether Hong Kong can serve as a reinsurance centre is equivalent to asking whether the ultimate risk bearers will want to locate in Hong Kong. For this question, a two-handed economist answer is as follows. On the one hand, the clustering of direct insurers and the infrastructure provided for brokerage activities in Hong Kong can act as a convenient front office market for reinsurers; in that sense, Hong Kong is a suitable location for reinsurers. On the other hand, the reinsurance business has not been that attractive in the Hong Kong environment, as is evidenced by the opinions of several reinsurers.

What about indigenous efforts, in other words, forming reinsurance companies from the ground up? This question must be examined from the perspective of Hong Kong's ability to raise funds and to maintain its position as a world financial centre after 1997. More precisely, Hong Kong's advantage lies in its ability to raise additional capital through the stock market. But insurance companies in Hong Kong have not typically been organized as stock corporations. The only insurance company that has publicly traded stocks in Hong Kong is National Mutual. Aside from this revealed preference of most Hong Kong insurance companies not to go public, any indigenous effort to raise capital for insurance companies must depend to some extent on the listing requirement of the Hong Kong Stock Exchange, generally and more particularly for insurance companies. There are immense organizational problems that will take great vision and skill to solve. In short, the availability of financial infrastructure is not sufficient to make Hong Kong necessarily a suitable place for raising capital for reinsurance. A human mind must make the first move.

Hong Kong as a potential world reinsurance centre cannot be discussed without taking into account the presence of China as the backdrop. In an ordinary situation, it is not good economics to believe that an emerging insurance market should develop its reinsurance business; a country that demands risk protection cannot be the same country that exports risk protection. To do so would violate the principle of comparative advantage. The idea that by developing reinsurance, a country's balance of payment can somehow be improved is also a misconception. Yet, in the case of the relationship between China and Hong Kong, it could be argued that there is room for risk-shifting. The disparity between the financial strengths of the two areas implies a good reason for the exchange of risk. Reinsurers located in Hong Kong can offer reinsurance contracts not only to insurers in Hong Kong but also to insurers in Mainland China. Hong Kong people's linguistic, cultural, and geographical advantage will afford reinsurers a better understanding of the potential clients (partners) in China than others might have. Such an understanding is very important in establishing a reinsurance business, because the reinsurers have to trust the insurers in order to control moral hazard and adverse selection problems.

Of course, identifying the underlying reason for an exchange does not imply that the *institution* established for the exchange will necessarily be efficient. In the case of Hong Kong and China, a recent three-point proposal offered by Mr. Kenneth Ng of the China Reinsurance Co. (HK) Ltd. is a starting point for the shaping of policies for a design of such an institution.[31] Specifically, Mr. Ng requested that the Hong Kong government to (a) grant tax exemption status for offshore/overseas profit, (b) grant tax exemption on equalization funds — funds set aside to meet future claims, and (c) provide human resources training for insurance at the tertiary level of education. The proposal is understandable from the point of view of the insurance industry. However, this may not have touched on the heart of the issue.

Industry practitioners need to be aware of the fact that any industry in Hong Kong can request tax relief. There is no reason to believe a *priori* that the insurance industry should deserve preferential treatment. Therefore, factors must be identified to illustrate the peculiar aspects of overseas linkages and interactions in the insurance business. Otherwise, the insurance industry will have difficulty explaining why it, rather than other industries, needs subsidization in the form of tax relief. The government cannot subsidize all industries, and in the absence of convincing reasoning, subsidies are seldom granted.[32]

Captives

Although captives can also be reinsurers, the underlying reason for forming captives is quite different from that for forming reinsurance companies. A captive is a form of self insurance for multinational corporations which can exist even without tax concession. The reason for this may be because of transaction costs (see Chapter 2). Forming a captive is like vertically integrating a business; there is nothing unusual about this in the organisation structure of a company. Most captive centres of the world, however, thrive on their successes based on tax advantages. It is for

Table 5.2(a)
Captive Insurance Company Distribution

Location of Owners		Country	
Bermuda	103	U.S.	88
Guernsey	44	U.K.	84
Isle of Man	22	Sweden	18
Luxembourg	21	Australia	12
U.K.	11	France	8
Singapore	10	Canada	5
Vermont	8	Finland	5
Cayman Islands	6	Various	5
Barbados	4	Japan	4
Australia	3	Switzerland	4
Germany	3	Germany	4
Michigan	2	Denmark	3
Norway	2	Norway	2
Finland	2	European	2
France	1	South Africa	1
Hong Kong	1	Eire (Ireland)	1
Maryland	1	New Zealand	1
Netherlands Antilles	1	Belgium	1
Sweden	1	The Netherlands	1
Florida	1		
Tennessee	1		
Delaware	1		
Total	249	Total	249

Source : Bawcutt, P.A., *Captive Insurance Companies*, Woodhead-Faulkner. 3rd ed.,1991. Appendix 1.

this reason that the term "captives" sometimes also carries the negative and possibly unjustifiable connotation of tax evasion.

There are currently 3,600 captives in the world, 800 of which are group captives. The rest are single parent captives. Most of the demand for captives come from the U.S. (about 50%) and the U.K. (about 25%) (see Table 5.2). About 25% of the world's captives are formed in Bermuda.[33] Bermuda has 62% of the captive sponsor origin from the U.S.; the Cayman Islands have 86.5% of captive

Table 5.2(b)
Top Twelve Countries of Captive Sponsor Origin

U.S.	1,922
U.K.	512
Canada	147
Sweden	107
France	65
Australia	50
Netherlands	49
Japan	46
Switzerland	35
Belgium	31
Germany	29
Norway	23

Source : Ramming, Corinne, "The Captive Scene Around the Globe," *Global Reinsurance*, March–May 1996
Note: Figures are number of captives.

origin from the U.S. and Canada. Probably because of this, entities within American territory, such as the U.S. Virgin Islands, Vermont, Georgia, Illinois, Delaware, Tennessee, Colorado, and Hawaii have all joined in the competition by offering their own captive laws.[34]

Hong Kong currently houses an insignificant proportion of the world's captives. The thing to note about captive centres is that it takes many years to build a reputation. Bermuda began housing captives in 1930 and only acquired its niche in 1960. Without the participation of innovative insurers such as ACE and EXEL in the 1980s and Mid Ocean Re in the 1990s, the island would not have been able to acquire its leading position in the field of captives.[35] For British Virgin Islands, it took about thirty years (starting in 1960) to build into what it is today — the home of 151,000 IBC companies.[36]

There are several difficulties associated with developing Hong Kong into a world insurance captive centre. Aside from the fact that it would be starting late, the severe competition from established centres would necessitate Hong Kong putting out extra marketing efforts in order to build a niche in this area. Establishing Hong Kong as an insurance captive centre cannot be justified purely as a business proposition, although there would certainly be spill-over effects to the rest of the economy. The minimum amount of capital and surplus required to set up a captive in Bermuda is only US$120,000 (less than HK$1 million). Indeed, the regulatory supervision required for captives may be the opposite of that required for the reinsurance business. The former requires low capital and surplus with a hands-off policy; the latter requires high capital and surplus with a hands-on policy. Experienced captive centres such as Bermuda know how to strike a balance. As of 1994, the island had attracted a total capital and surplus of US$29.8 billion from international insurance and reinsurance companies.[37] Hong Kong will have much catching up to do if it wants to compete.

Hong Kong also lacks the "turquoise waters, mountains, and emerald golf courses" of other captives — important ingredients for luring CEOs and managers to meetings and conferences. Hong Kong has its own attractions, of course, but ultimately, it is the potential for doing business, the trust a company can have in the regulators, and the human resources that can be utilized that would make a difference if multinationals were to choose it as a site for their captives. Bermuda is said to have a "reputation for probity"; and captives centres on the whole are known to have "open, flexible regulators".[38] Whatever these terms may mean, and whatever it takes for the regulators to attract potential captives, the 1997 issue will no doubt cloud the local government's efforts to market the concept. As with all business activities, when it comes to the bottom line, credibility could be more important than water, mountains, and the surrounding rest and recreational activities.

In the face of these obstacles, Hong Kong's best option may be to model itself after the U.S. Virgin Islands (USVI). As an unincorporated territory of the U.S., USVI occupies a unique status. Being part of the U.S., it has the U.S. Congress-approved authority to enact legislation for tax exempt companies. Although the island has a high degree of autonomy, USVI captives can nevertheless insure employee benefits under the Employee Retirement Income Security Act (ERISA), a piece of continental legislature that has the effect of encouraging pension funds to turn over their asset management to insurance companies (see further elaboration on this issue in the next section on MPF). This means that USVI captives may also be entitled to the protection of the Pension Benefit Guarantee Corporation (Penny Benny) in the U.S. However, USVI captives cannot engage in trade or business in the continental U.S. unless they also elect to be taxed as a U.S. corporation under section 953(d) of the U.S. tax code. The relationship is complicated indeed. But this is exactly the kind of thing future Hong Kong legislators will need to sort out with the Mainland Chinese government after 1997.

MPF Factor

In 1995 the Hong Kong government enacted a Mandatory Provident Fund Ordinance (MPF) with subsidiary legislation scheduled for completion by early 1997. The MPF is a form of *forced* savings that requires both employees and employers to contribute an amount equal to 5% of an employee's earnings to a retirement fund[39]. The plan is to be run privately, under competition. Trustees of the fund are to be governed by the laws of Hong Kong and the MPF Schemes Authority which also monitors the maintenance of the scheme standards. It is estimated that the MPF scheme will generate a savings pool worth HK$20 billion to HK$40 billion a year.

Competition for the funds generated from the MPF is expected to be intense. On this effort, the insurance industry trust emphasizes the extra benefits it could offer relative to what pension management funds can offer.[40] This should not be difficult. The profitability of pension management funds in Hong Kong has not been particularly impressive. Many Hong Kong pension funds have failed to keep up with inflation, and some even suffered losses in 1995, a year in which the stock market is supposed to have performed extremely well. A study of 295 pension schemes conducted by Wyatt Co. found that the median performing Hong Kong pension fund returned 4.7% (about half the rate of inflation) in the 12 months leading up to September 1995. With a total of HK$51.3 billion under management, the top performing fund produced returns of more than 24%, while the worst performer lost about 12%.[41] According to Tower Perrin's study, the territory's three biggest managers — HSBC Asset Management, Jardine Fleming, and Schroders — which account for about 55% of the total retirement market, were outpaced by a computer-generated benchmark that tracks index movements.[42]

Another factor that works in favour of the insurances companies is that a typical consumer would not be able to differentiate between different investment funds, all of which claim that they can produce the best results for the MPF fund. There was a general lack of knowledge about the subject. At the time when the ordinance was passed, a survey of 1,000 Hong Kong citizens aged fifteen to sixty-four conducted by Prudential (an insurance company) revealed that only 32% of the respondents knew that the government has passed the MPF legislation, and 62% acknowledged that employees had to contribute to the fund. Among those who knew that employees had to contribute, only 42% knew that they would have to contribute 5% of their earnings. More than half of the respondents (55%) believed that the MPF would be unable to help them meet their retirement needs. Among the group that held this belief, 64% were currently raising children, 62% were between thirty and thirty-nine years old, and 60% were married. Of the respondents. 25% indicated that if they had the choice, they would not participate in the MPF.[43]

Insurance products, in principle, have a certain competitive edge over retirement products. Life insurance with large savings components may be a good buy for many people, because it guarantees a saving rate on cash surrender value with a variable bonus in addition to providing life insurance before retirement. For a worker who has a monthly income of HK$10,000, the amount accumulated in the MFP after he has worked for ten years will last approximately only one or two years after the person retires. Life insurance companies can offer similar pay-offs with protection even before retirement. In addition, there is a service aspect of life insurance in that insurance company agents are expected to provide a more personal service than that which pension funds and banks may be able to offer.

Although insurance products in principle hold an edge over retirement funds, the actual products offered by an insurance company can be different. Indeed, no theory can perfectly determine which organization will be most efficient at handling the society's savings and long-term investment. Much of that depends on the effort each institution expends as promotion as well as the policies adopted by the government. In the U.S., the life insurance business shrank significantly between the 1960s and the late 1970s due to the emergence of private pension funds. The general public no longer saw the need to use life insurance as a form of savings but considered buying both term insurance and a pension to be a better substitute.[44] However, as a result of the enactment of the Employee Retirement Income Security Act (ERISA) in 1974, which encouraged pension funds to turn over fund management to life insurance companies, life insurance companies in the U.S. began to restructure their business to become managers of assets for pension funds. Nowadays, more than half of the assets managed by life insurance companies in the U.S. are for pension funds and not for life insurance. The market share of life insurance companies as a percentage of total financial intermediary assets has increased accordingly since 1980.[45]

In Hong Kong's case, the relative competitiveness of pension funds and insurance companies cannot be predetermined at this early stage of their development. However, in evaluating the competitive position of insurance companies versus pension funds, several are anticipated to be of importance:

(1) Investment Philosophies: It is a common practice to compare the investment performance of a fund in terms of past performance. However, this can be misleading. Neither a high nor a low investment performance of a particular company can suggest anything about its long-term potential. The theory of rational

expectation in economics would support this line of thinking. Indeed, in a 1996 seminar run by Watson-Wyatt on fund performance in Hong Kong, a company analyst suggested that there was a need to go "soft" in fund performance evaluations. What the speaker meant is that there is non-quantitative information about a fund that needs to be taken into considerations in evaluating its performance. Human character, investment philosophies, and the organizational structure of the fund can all make a difference.

(2) Management of interest and exchange rate risk: A fund manager not only has to look for profitable opportunities, he must also provide effective risk management. A manager of mutual funds may be quite good in terms of his risk diversification ability, but his risk management ability may be low. Nowadays, financial derivatives such as forward contracts, financial futures, and various types of options and swaps exist for risk diversification purpose. These are sophisticated risk management techniques that may or may not be suitable for achieving long-term investment objectives. Indeed, misuses of financial derivatives can lead to an increase rather than a decrease in risk.[46] The Mandatory Provident Fund Office of Hong Kong, in specifying the limitations of the investment of pension funds, states that the "use of derivatives [is allowed] for hedging purposes only".[47] However, it would be difficult to enforce this provision. Ultimately, the burden of proof is on the enforcement agent and not on the fund manager.

(3) Duration Matching: An important risk management method that is particularly relevant for institutions or funds dealing with long-term investment is asset-liability duration matching. The method is more commonly used by banks and can be performed in terms of either an income gap or a duration gap analysis.[48] However, for risk management purposes, it may be relevant for pension fund and insurance fund management, as well. Briefly, the duration of a portfolio of securities is the weighted average of the duration of the individual securities, with the weights reflecting each security's percentage in the total portfolio of assets. Banks use this to figure out the effect of interest-rate changes on their net worth by calculating the average duration for assets and for

liabilities. Conceptually, if the duration of assets matches the duration of liabilities, there will not be an interest rate risk on the net worth of the company. For pension and insurance funds, similar management techniques apply. It is, however, up to an individual pension fund manager or individual insurance company to choose a particular method.

(4) Insolvency protection: The possibility that a pension fund or an insurance company will go bankrupt cannot be ignored. How the industries would handle such a situation, and how the government's view on this issue, will effect the competitive positions of the two sectors. While certain guaranty funds – those provided by the Motor Insurers' Bureau for third-party liability insurance and by the Employees' Compensation Assistance Scheme for employees' compensation – already exist in the Hong Kong insurance industry, no guaranty funds exist for life insurance and for the pension funds that life insurance companies manage. The Mandatory Provident Fund Authority is proposing that a Compensation Fund be set up for the MPF scheme. Its similarity to the Pension Benefit Guarantee Corporation (Penny Benny) in the U.S., and its differential effects (if any) on pension funds versus insurance companies in Hong Kong can only be ascertainable in the future.[49]

Looking ahead, the insurance industry can benefit if the following positions are adopted: First, life insurance can be used as a substitute for mandatory savings. Individuals should be allowed to choose whatever form of savings they prefer, even if saving is "mandatory." Second, a more transparent policy on insurance investment and risk management strategies would be useful. Not only would it result in the increased confidence of policyholders, but insurance companies would be able to use the opportunity to demonstrate an edge over retirement funds managers. Third, institutional designs to curb moral hazard on the MPF Compensation Fund are effective. A free market principle applied to the use of a public fund is bound to result in severe moral hazard and adverse selection problems that will come back to haunt the industry and the regulators. An understanding and designing a curb on such possibilities therefore can benefit the industry.

Summary

Hong Kong's competitive advantage can be built upon the territory's ability to provide institutional development and strategic alliances in the area. Already, a trend towards co-operation is developing between insurance industries and other sectors of the economy such as the banking industry. Additional development between Hong Kong and other regions in terms of locality and types of insurance can occur as well. In terms of forming alliances with the China market, the potential of joint ventures, reinsurance, and captives possibilities have been explored. While a market niche may be difficult to secure, the availability of a large savings fund may allow the insurance industry to further expand its investment and marketing potential. Regulators should not stand in the way of these trends, and may indeed want to adopt a more proactive stance in certain cases. Caution needs to be exercised, however, in order to guard against the moral hazard and adverse selection problems that might be by-products of such developments.

Notes

1. Speech delivered at the Symposium on Service Promotion: *Hong Kong Into the 21st Century: The Servicing Economy,* 12 March 1996.
2. Santomero and Chung (1992), however, demonstrated that the combined firms are statistically more stable than are their independent counterparts.
3. The *Glass-Steagall Act* in the U.S. was enacted in 1933. It prohibited commercial banks from underwriting or dealing in corporate securities, including those of the insurance companies. There has been much discussion about appealing the act in recent years.

4. Deposit insurance in the U.S., while it provides deposit security for bank customers, have also led to many moral hazard problems. Pundits in the U.S. banking industry have sometimes argued that the insurance provided by the FDIC is for the banking industry, and not for the insurance industry. The "source of strength" of an insurance-banking combination is in the banking industry.

5. A review of the development of bancassurance in seven countries can be found in *Bancassurance*, Scor Tech, December 1993. According to the figures provided by Mr. Lawrence Churchill of NatWest Life & Investment Services, NatWest UK, the market share of bancassurance rose from 7% of the Life and Pensions market in 1990 to 16% in 1994 in England. In France, the corresponding share increased from 39% in 1990 to 52% in 1994.

6. A more recent example is AIG's acquisition of SPC Credit Ltd., a medium-sized Hong Kong finance company previously owned by Bank America Corp., as reported in *Asia & Pacific Insurance Newsletter*, February 1996.

7. The Asian Development Bank and the Finance Ministry of PRC, for example, recently appointed the Australian Social Security Department to study this issue.

8. Article from *The Hong Kong Standard*, 5 December 1995. The exchange rate of yuan and U.S. dollar was roughly 10 to 1.

9. Based on the figure provided in a speech made by Mr. Pan Lufu, Executive Vice Chairman of Insurance Institute of China (IIC), "Present and Future of China's Insurance Market," 24 April 1996, in Hong Kong.

10. Article from *South China Morning Post*, 14 December 1995.

11. Article from *The Hong Kong Standard*, 8 December 1995.

12. Whereas in Taiwan the penetration rate is 58.6%, according to a survey taken in 1995. Article from *China Times*, 28 December 1995.

13. Article from *Ta Kung Pao*, 6 December 1995

14. *China Insurance Market, 1996.*

15. Speech by Mr. Pan Lufu, ibid.

16. A step-by-step guide can be found in *China Insurance Market, 1996.*

17. A representative position of foreign insurers' entry into the insurance markets in Asia, including China, can be found in a speech by Mr. Douglas C. Henck of Aetna International in a recent conference, "Opening Insurance Markets in Emerging Economies: Striking a Balance", 25 March 1996.

18. According to a newspaper report in China, PICC has eighty-one foreign branch offices scattered all over the world, including the U.S., Europe and Hong Kong, article from *Shenzhen SEZ Daily*, 8 December 1995
19. Descriptions of these companies as well as of the national ones can be found in chapter 7 of *China Insurance Market, 1996.*
20. The news was reported in the *HK Economic Journal* on 8 May 1996. The statement in the text is an interpretation of the strategy rather an announcement of the company's strategy.
21. The notion of comparative advantage here is that of Schumpeterian rather than Ricardian where endowment is assumed to be given.
22. As mentioned in the last chapter on regulation, the formulation of these policies are currently taking place through informal "Three Regions" functions and events.
23. *Commissioner's Annual Report, 1995,* p. 15. The retention ratios of different types of insurance are: accident and health, 86.6%; motor vehicle, 75.4%; goods in transit, 62.2%; property damage, 53.6%, general liability, 65.6%; and miscellaneous, 36.7%.
24. For example, Malaysia, Singapore, and Thailand all had net retention ratios higher than 70% in 1993.
25. See the discussion in the theoretical chapter and the reinsurance chart in Figure 4.2 of Chapter 4.
26. Based on the interview conducted by *Oriental Daily News* with Mr. George Leung of SCOR, 15 March 1996.
27. Data derived from Sigma, presented in a speech by Mr. Wolfgang Droste of Cologne Reinsurance Company, Germany, "Reinsurance developments worldwide and in Asia – developments and prospects." 27 March, 1996, Hong Kong.
28. Based on a speech by Mr. Frank Speight of Lloyd's of London in the International Summit on Emerging Asian Insurance Markets, March 1996, Hong Kong.
29. Speech by Mr. Wolfgang Droste, op. cit.
30. This position has been articulated by Ho (1995). Similarly, Mr. David A. Rosier of the Reinsurance Group of America, Hong Kong, also indicated, "The issue nowadays with reinsurers is not simply capacity – a reinsurer can offer so much more in return for a representative share of the business and the local environment has to be able to accommodate this for the benefit of all parties." Speech made in March 1996, Hong Kong.
31. "To Promote Hong Kong as a World Class Reinsurance Center in the 21st

Century", paper presented at the Symposium on Services Promotion, 12 March 1996.

32. The point about human resource training will be addressed to in the next chapter.

33. In 1995, 900 of the total licensed insurers in Bermuda fell into Class I (companies writing only the risks of their parents "US on/offshore or sponsors) and Class II (captives writing no more than 20% unrelated business." See "US On/Offshore Captive Insurance Review", p. 73, *Global Reinsurance*, March–May 1996.

34. Ibid., p. 73–116.

35. "Market Report: Bermuda", by Johnathan Evans, *The Review*, September 1995.

36. The name IBC is derived from the International Business Company Act of 1984,"Virgin Territory", by Justin Wood, *International Risk Management,* July/August 1995.

37. *Global Reinsurance*, March–May 1996, p.96.

38. ibid.

39. The earnings subject to the MPF contribution have a minimum level of $4,000/month and a maximum cap of $20,000/month.It will cover employees of aged eighteen to sixty-four, including self-employed persons. The benefits are supposed to be fully vested, to be portable, and to be paid in a lump sum at age sixty-five.

40. Insurance company can also manage retirement funds. This create competition between companies (insurance and pension funds companies,) not competitions between products (insurance products and pension funds products).

41. *Measurement of Investment Performance Survey for Hong Kong Retirement Schemes, Annual Report 1995*, Watson-Wyatt Worldwide. See also the comments in *South China Morning Post*, 19 December 1995.

42. Article from *South China Morning Post*, 21 April 1996

43. Article from *HK Economic Journal*, 19 December 1995.

44. Cummings (1975), p. 42, reported that in the U.S., savings through life insurance companies (measured as a percentage of total net acquisitions of financial assets by households) declined from 21.8% in 1954 to 11.1% in 1973.

45. See Mishkin (1995), p. 348, Table 1.

46. The huge financial loss suffered through derivatives transaction in the

case of Barings is a case in point. Similarly, the trading of futures in Mainland China, though established originally as a risk reduction device, has subjected itself to the speculative attack that the market was put to a halt in recent years.

47. *What is MPF?* p.16.
48. Mishkin (1995), chp. 6, pp. 402–413.
49. It is important to note that since the establishment of Penny Benny, the number of pension funds has more than doubled in the U.S., and yet the number of federal audits of pension plans has declined. Allegedly, fewer than 1% of the private plans insured by Penny Benny are audited each year. Penny Benny's liability is estimated to have exceed its assets by more than US$15 billion in 1995. Mishkin (1995), p. 357.

CHAPTER 6

Public Perception and Trust: The Case of Life Insurance

Our final area of investigation has to do with the public's perception of insurance products and the companies supplying them. Since insurance is primarily a people's business, the issue has much to do with training and education of the practitioners. Although under the topic of training and education, general insurance will also be discussed, the bulk of this chapter is devoted to the discussion of life insurance.

There are reasons to believe that life insurance has a special place in regard to the public's perception. First, it is often argued that life insurance is a form of savings. Some theoretical models go far in demonstrating that life insurance products can have an implicit rate of interest higher than that of alternative forms of saving.[1] Whether the public in fact views life insurance products in this way is an interesting question. Second, life insurance products are different from non-life products in that the beneficiary is not the policyholder himself or herself. In other words, purchasing life insurance can sometimes be rationalized only if there is a bequest motive, that is, the insured must value something beyond his life in order for such a purchase to make sense. In this sense, the public's willingness to pay for life insurance can be more than just a present value calculation.[2] Third, there is something to the dictum that "life insurance can only be sold but not bought." Clearly, the social status, the appearance, and the business ethics of a sales force reflect the image an insurance company wants to portray to its clients. Thus, public perception is more important for life insurance than it is for non-life insurance.

Theoretically, sales efforts for life and non-life products are also different. Agents for life insurance products are sometimes viewed as performing the unique role of persuader. Persuasion is arguably less necessary when it comes to selling general insurance than it is for selling life insurance. The management of business risk has few emotional elements. Corporate demand for insurance services is guided by profit motives. The need for risk management is automatically revealed in a corporation's attempt to succeed in the face of competition (Alchian 1950). Even though alternative risk-diversifying devices are available in the financial market as substitutes for insurance, there is demand for insurance services beyond its use for risk diversification, as described in Mayers and Smith (1982). Consumer demand for insurance, on the other hand, has a larger persuasion component. Individuals who do not worry about themselves or others will have little need for the risk transfer function provided by insurance. The extent to which people worry about risk exposure of various types depends on their risk aversion and on their feelings towards others (especially in the case of life insurance). However, it might be the case that individuals will behave in a risk-averse manner only when they are fully aware of the risks they face. This is exactly what was said earlier. Persuasion on the part of life insurance agents may indeed have a specific purpose that is not replaceable by direct sales methods, and for this reason, the issue of public perception is particularly important.

General Approach to the Question of Public Perception

We approach the life insurance question from the general public's perspective by asking: (1) What is the nature of the demand for life insurance in Hong Kong? (2) To what extent does the Hong Kong public rely on insurance as a form of savings? (3) To what extent does the Hong Kong public trust insurance companies and insurance agents? And (4) To what extent can the professional image of the industry be improved?

For understandable reasons, the insurance companies of Hong Kong often want to guard their company's information, especially when it concerns the demographics and the socioeconomic characteristics of the company's actual and potential customers. An initial attempt to form a very general picture of the aggregate distribution of the monthly premium of existing life insurance policyholders in Hong Kong had to be aborted due to the difficulty in obtaining co-operation from the industry. An independent opinion survey therefore was conducted through the Social Science Research Center of the University of Hong Kong. While opinion surveys run into methodological problems of selectivity bias and truthful revelations, the general picture may nevertheless provide a glimpse into the public's view of the life insurance industry in Hong Kong.[3]

The public opinion survey was directed towards heads of households as a way to gain access to people who need life insurance for the "real" purpose that the product is supposed to serve (as opposed to those who buy life insurance for the purpose of doing their agent-friend a favour). Particularly as a result of some of the alleged tactics of life insurance agents, some people believe that the premium a policyholder pays does not always measure his real need for insurance. Such a payment can be made in exchange for favours or simply to get an agent-friend off one's back. The position of this study is that this may or may not be an accurate picture of what occurs when a person decides to buy life insurance. However, it is less likely to happen in the case of heads of households, who must manage the risk of the whole family.

The head of the household is defined as the person who contributes the most income to and handles the most expenses of the household. He or she was asked to respond to a questionnaire, which is divided into three parts. Part A is for respondents who have bought life insurance products in the past. Part B is for respondents who have not bought life insurance products. In theory, those who answer questions in one section will not answer questions in the other, but all respondents will answer the questions in either part A or part B. In reality, however, it is possible that a respondent may not answer the questions in either section, because he might have bought a life insurance policy at one time in the past but have cancelled it by the time the survey was conducted. All respondents also have to answer some socioeconomic and demographic questions at the beginning of the survey, and at the end, in part C.

The order in which questions are asked is not the same as the order in which the results are to be analysed. The questions in the questionnaire are ordered to provide a smooth transition from one question to another. Considerable planning was required before the survey was conducted, taking the psychology of the respondents and their need for privacy into account in designing the choice of words in each question. The questions in part A ask whether the respondent has bought a life insurance policy with a saving component, and if so, whether he would rely on the life insurance policy as his retirement income, and how much he pays per month in life insurance policy premiums (counting both life and term insurance). The latter question is posed for the purpose of obtaining an aggregate distribution of monthly premium, which we were at one point trying to obtain from insurance companies. Theoretically, at least, this data together with a question in part C concerning the respondents' *willingness to pay* as a percentage of their income can potentially generate an income distribution of people who buy life insurance. If one makes a simplifying assumption that people spend a fixed amount of their income on life insurance, premium distribution in fact reflects income distribution. The purpose of the exercise is to see if the penetration rate of a particular income group is high or low compared to the average. It may be interesting to find out whether people in a low-income group buy life insurance as often as do those in a high-income group. A related set of questions are also asked concerning the respondent's purchase of his or her family members' insurance policies. It is possible that someone does not buy an insurance policy for himself or herself, but may buy others' policies, of which he or she is the beneficiary. If a respondent buys policies for others, the questionnaire also asks for whom among the family members has the insurance been bought. If more than one insurance is bought, using the highest premium insurance as the basis for comparision, and how much the monthly premium is.

In part B, which is for respondents who have not bought life insurance, the questionnaire asks for a list of reasons for which they have chosen not to do so. It may be that the respondents think there are better substitutes for life insurance, that they do not trust insurance agents, and so on. Finally, in part C, the questionnaire asks about the percentage of income the respondent is willing to save, and the percentage of income the respondent is willing to spend on life insurance premium. A telephone survey, conducted in Cantonese with a standardized format, was completed over a two-day period on May 23 and May 24, 1996. Five hundred and eighty observations were collected and analysed.

Survey Result 1: Penetration Rate

Out of 580 households, 290 chose to answer questions in part A while 274 chose part B. This suggests that out of a random sample of 564 heads of households in Hong Kong, 51.4% have bought life insurance either for themselves or for others in the family. This figure is higher than the 40% penetration rate that has often been quoted for the life insurance market in Hong Kong. The latter figure was reached based on the number of policies in existence (as recorded by the Insurance Authority) divided by the total population of Hong Kong. The discrepancy between the penetration rate in our survey and the official rate could reflect two things: (1) our sample concentrates on heads of households, who are more likely to buy life insurance, and (2) there may be individuals who buy life insurance from overseas markets. The latter possibility also suggests that the actual penetration rate of life insurance in the Hong Kong market could very well be higher than the officially quoted rate of 40%.

A way of further addressing the question of penetration is to segregate the sample into two groups — one that holds foreign passports, and the other that doesn't. Overseas purchases are more likely to be made by those in the foreign passport-holder group.

Table 6.1

Penetration Rates as a Function of Socioeconomic Characteristics, 1996 Survey

	Have you bought life insurance?		Number of Respondents	Penetration Ratio
	Yes	No		
Immigration Status				
With foreign passport	42	28	70	0.60
Without foreign passport	239	234	473	0.51
Residence District				
Wan Chai	7	7	14	0.50
Hong Kong Island East	26	17	43	0.61
Hong Kong Island Central and West	17	20	37	0.46
Hong Kong Island South	11	11	22	0.50
Kwun Tong	33	34	67	0.49
Kowloon City	10	16	26	0.38
Wong Tai Sin	10	16	26	0.38
Mong Kok	11	18	29	0.38
Sham Shui Po	6	9	15	0.40
Yau Ma Tei and Tsim Sha Tsui	22	18	40	0.55
Sha Tin	45	23	68	0.66
Tsuen Wan	12	7	19	0.63
Kwai Tsing	15	12	27	0.56
Tuen Mun	23	11	34	0.68
Yuen Long	16	10	26	0.62
New Territories North	11	13	24	0.46
Tai Po	10	6	16	0.63
Type of Housing				
Public	107	114	221	0.48
Home Ownership Scheme	41	23	64	0.64
Private	119	103	222	0.54
Village	6	5	11	0.55
Occupation				
Manager or executive	32	17	49	0.65
Professional	45	25	70	0.64
Assistant professional	11	8	19	0.58
Clerk	53	41	94	0.56
Servicing or salesperson	60	42	102	0.59
Craftsman or similar occupation	18	12	30	0.60
Factory worker	18	13	31	0.58
Non-technical	19	31	50	0.38
Homemaker	12	19	31	0.39
Age				
<= 25	20	26	46	0.43
25 < age <= 35	118	73	191	0.62
35 < age <= 45	100	73	173	0.58
45 < age <= 55	25	34	59	0.42
> 55	27	68	95	0.28

Indeed, the penetration rate of insurance in the foreign passport-holder group (70 respondents) was 60%, whereas the penetration rate in the non-foreign passport holder group (473 respondents) was 50.5%. The penetration rates calculated on the basis of residence location, type of residence, occupation, and age brackets are listed in Table 6.1. The general pattern was quite revealing: Hong Kong Island East, Sha Tin, Tuen Mun, Yuen Long, and Tai Po all have penetration rates of more than 60%. Respondents living in public housing have the lowest penetration rate, and respondents living in home ownership schemes have the highest penetration rate. Professionals have a higher penetration rate than do non-professionals, those in the twenty-five- to forty-year-old age group have a higher penetration rate than do either the younger or the older group, with the twenty-five- to thirty-five-year-old age group having the highest penetration rate. It is interesting to note that the highest "refuse to answer" rate for the question asking whether or not respondents have bought life insurance for themselves or other members of the family was among those fifty-five years old and above.

Survey Result 2: Demand for Life Insurance

Four questions in the questionnaire involve various characteristics of the demand for life insurance products in Hong Kong. The first, directed to all 580 respondents, asked how much a respondent is willing to spend a month on life insurance premium. While 276 (47.6%) of those surveyed chose not to respond to this question, of the 304 who responded, 46 (15%) said they would not spend any amount per month to buy life insurance. The number is interesting in that when it is compared with the aggregate penetration rate of 51.4%, it suggests that more than half of the people who have not bought life insurance are actually willing to pay for some amount of life insurance. The figure can also be used as a type of benchmark figure for the saturation level of the life insurance market in Hong Kong. One might expect that in every society, there will be a certain number of people who will not buy insurance no matter what. If so,

Table 6.2
Frequency Distribution of Monthly Premium of the Respondents
(Total number of observations = 221)

Monthly Premium x	Frequency	Percentage	Cumulative Percentage
$x = 0$	39	17.65	17.65
$x <= 100$	7	3.17	20.82
$100 < x <= 200$	17	7.69	28.51
$200 < x <= 300$	31	14.03	42.54
$300 < x <= 400$	25	11.31	53.85
$400 < x <= 500$	56	25.34	79.19
$500 < x <= 600$	21	9.50	88.69
$600 < x <= 700$	10	4.52	93.21
$700 < x <= 800$	11	4.98	98.19
$800 < x <= 900$	4	1.81	100.00

that percentage will be the upper bound of market penetration.

The remaining 258 respondents, who answered the willingness to pay question positively, indicated that they would be willing to pay between 1% and 20% of their monthly income for life insurance premium, with 10 people (3.9%) reporting a willingness to pay over 20% of their income (which may possibly reflect a misinterpretation of the question). The distribution is bimodal, with spikes occurring at 5% and 10% of the respondents' monthly income.

The second question was directed to those who answered only part A of the questionnaire. Most of the 290 who answered this section had bought life insurance for themselves, but 26 (9%) said they had bought life insurance for other members of their family but not for themselves. The survey also asked the group which had bought life insurance for themselves to give the monthly premium they are paying. While 40 (15.3%) of the respondents refused to answer, 221 gave numerical answers to the question. The frequency distribution is reported in Table 6.2.

The third question, which is aimed at understanding the demand for life insurance, asks respondents why they have *not* bought life insurance. Obviously, the question is directed only to respondents who answered questions in part B, meaning 274 of the 580 respondents. At the outset, only 5 (1.8%) of those who had not bought life insurance had not been contacted by insurance agents or salespersons. While it is true that the respondent's interpretation of the term "contact" may be so broad as to include any advertisements, television commercials, billboards, and friends of friends. The figure suggests that if a respondent had not purchased life insurance, it was not because he or she didn't know about it. There was no lack of effort to educate the public on the part of the life insurance companies. Life insurance concepts are very familiar to most Hong Kong people,[4] but contact is apparently not enough; it is persuasion that will influence the purchase decision of the consumer.

Life insurance companies may also be pleased to know that it is not because people don't trust insurance companies that they have not bought life insurance. Only 27 (9.85%) of the respondents selected "distrust of insurance companies" as their reason for not buying life insurance. The most popular answer was "cannot afford it", which was chosen by 80 respondents (29.2%) and "other reasons", which was chosen by 61 respondents (22.3%). "No ideal beneficiary", "already have other life risk protection method", and "still looking for a good policy" were all answers selected by a small percentage of the respondents.

Finally, a question was directed to those who had bought life insurance for others. Of the respondents to part A, 162 of the 290 had bought insurance for others in their family. Using the family member whose policy has the highest premium as the basis for the question, 87 (53.7%) of the respondents had bought insurance for their spouses, 29 (17.9%) had bought insurance for their sons/daughters, 16 (9.9%) had bought insurance for their parents, while the remaining 30 (18.5%) had bought insurance for others.[5] Among the life insurance products bought, 134 (82.7%) had saving components, and 24 (14.8%) were term insurance. When asked

Table 6.3
Frequency Distribution of Monthly Premium of Insurance for others in the family of the respondent
(Total number of observations = 130)

Monthly Premium x	Frequency	Percentage	Cumulative Percentage
x = 0	24	18.46	18.46
x <= 100	6	4.62	23.08
100 < x <= 200	19	14.62	37.70
200 < x <= 300	21	16.15	53.85
300 < x <= 400	11	8.46	62.31
400 < x <= 500	27	20.77	83.08
500 < x <= 600	12	9.23	92.31
600 < x <= 700	6	4.62	96.93
700 < x <= 800	3	2.31	99.24
800 < x <= 900	1	0.77	100.00

about the monthly premium of these policies, 31 (19.3%) respondents refused to answer, and 130 (80.7%) gave a numerical answer. The results are reported in Table 6.3.

Survey Result 3: Life Insurance as a Saving Channel

Of the 290 respondents who had bought life insurance either for themselves or for other members of the family, 192 (66.2%) said they would not rely on life insurance as a form of retirement income, and 73 (25.3%) said they would totally or partially rely on the life insurance policy they bought for retirement purposes. The 66.2% who said they would not rely on life insurance as a form of retirement income obviously include those who bought only term insurance, but they also include those who bought whole life insurance with no intention to save. The smaller percentage (25.3%) represented those who recognized that life insurance can be a form of retirement savings and might include those who bought only an endowment policy. However, this percentage is much higher than the official percentage of long-term endowment policy business in force in Hong Kong as recorded by the Insurance Authority. In 1993 only 183,283 of the 2,178,629 (8.4%) non-linked long-term policies in force were endowment policies.

Of the 261 respondents who bought life insurance for themselves, 216 (83%) had policies with saving components, and 37 (14.2%) bought only term insurance. Again, as compared with the term policy percentage officially recorded by the Insurance Authority, which classified 90,649 (4.2%) of the long-term policies as term insurance, the survey's percentage appeared a little higher. The survey also asked the group that bought life insurance for themselves to give the monthly premium they were paying. While 40 (15.3%) of the respondents refused to answer, 221 gave numerical answers to the question. The results were discussed in the previous section.

Of the 274 respondents who had not bought life insurance, 112 (40.9%) believed that regular saving was a better substitute for life insurance. The next most popular answer, chosen by 64 respondents (23.4%) was that real estate is a better substitute. Investment in securities and bonds as a substitute for insurance was selected by 19 respondents (7%). Interestingly, 7 respondents (3%) believed that gambling can be a substitute for life insurance. To this question, 51 respondents (18.6%) chose "don't know" or "hard to say," which could mean that the respondents had not really thought about the question before being surveyed.

Finally, regarding the question on the general pattern of saving , which was addressed to all 580 respondents, 270 (46.6%) refused to answer, and 87 (15%) said they had no savings. However, given that some of the same respondents indicated that they had bought life insurance, only 24 (8.3%) actually said that they had no savings. For those who saved, most indicated that they saved between 10% and 20% of their monthly income. Nineteen respondents (3.3%) reported a saving rate higher than 40%, suggesting a possible misinterpretation of the question. Comparing this distribution with that in an earlier question, one can also infer that a percentage of a respondent's savings is likely to have been spent on insurance premium. In any case, the question is only meant to generate an impression of the situation rather than to provide a scientific estimation of anything equivalent to the economists' notion of an average propensity to save.

Survey Result 4: Professional Image

As was pointed out in the previous section, the reason some respondents had not bought life insurance was not that they did not trust insurance companies. The general impression is that most customers do not interact with insurance companies directly but rather deal with agents. Two questions in the survey asked respondents to give their impressions of life insurance agents in Hong Kong. The question was deliberately biased in that it was only asked of respondents to part B. Presumably, people who had bought insurance products could not have felt too bad about their agents, or else they would not have bought the insurance in the first place. The survey could have directed the question to that group also, and the result is likely to be better. The methodology here is to first get the lower bound of this impression about the agents. If the lower bound is not too bad, then it is safe to say that the overall picture cannot be too bad, either.

For the first question, only 4 out of 265 respondents said they have a very good impression of insurance agents and salespersons. A much larger percentage, 129 out of 265 (48.7%), have a fair (average) impression of agents, while on the low end of the scale, 37 (13.9%) respondents ranked insurance agents as "pretty bad". However, as was mentioned previously, 56 respondents (21.1%) said that they had never been contacted by agents. A similar pattern was observed for the second question.

Public Perception of Insurance Agents

In addition to conducting the survey described above, the subject of public perception of insurance can also be approached from a different angle. The issue can also be analysed from the point of view of training and education, transparency in the operations of the insurance business, and the public image of insurance companies in their real concern for the society. All of these things have to do with the personalities and the images of individuals working in the industry. Theoretically speaking, banking and insurance are equally important financial sectors of any market economy; they provide complementary as well as substitute services. Yet, when it comes to the public's concept of the two sectors, most people think of banking as being somewhat superior to or more professional than insurance. This bias is an unfortunate one, and efforts should be made to correct it.

The crux of the problem may be that the insurance industry has never made it sufficiently clear to the public that it can be as effective as other financial institutions at handling investment and long-term savings. The activities of insurance companies in Hong Kong have to do in a large part with distribution. This is particularly true for the life insurance business. Life insurance agents have contributed a great deal to the success of the industry but they often appear to be only aware of the marketing aspect of their industry.

The problem partly arose because of how they were recruited. Typically, a life insurance agent is over eighteen years old, and need only a high school education. Recently, with the increased emphasis on the upgrading of agents' professional standards, more insurance companies are willing to employ university graduates. Practically speaking, knowledge has not been an important factor in the determination of an insurance agent's success. The financial success of an agent depends more on the social network he or she is able to cultivate. The personality, the social skills, and the network surrounding an agent are his or her biggest assets. In recruiting agents, many insurance companies have this in mind. It is therefore not uncommon for those over the age of thirty to leave a previous profession to become an insurance agent. For this group of agents, they do not need a university degree. They see periodically upgrading of practical knowledge to be more important.

Insurance Education and Training

Insurance education and training in Hong Kong concentrates on the practical aspects of selling insurance products. While insurance companies provide much of the in-house training for their sales agents, there are also other education and training channels available. The industry is not averse to general university degrees, but usually insurance diplomas and certificates are considered more practical. In the 1980s higher education in insurance could be acquired via post-secondary schools such as the Hong Kong Polytechnic. In the 1990s, with the elevation of that institution's status to the university level, insurance courses were gradually phased out. Training opportunities are now available largely through the Vocational Training Council (VTC) of the Hong Kong government. The VTC has an Insurance Training Board, which consists of members selected from various insurance associations, insurance companies, practitioners, educators and a labour and insurance commissioner, to periodically "assess the manpower and training needs of the insurance industry and to recommend to the VTC for the development of training facilities to meet the demand for trained insurance personnel".[6]

Over the last few years, insurance courses have been conducted at the Hong Kong Technical College (Chai Wan), the Kwun Tong Technical Institute, and the Insurance Training Centre of the VTC. These training institutions offer diploma courses and higher diploma courses on insurance in addition to short courses and professional seminars to help enhance the professional skills of practitioners. According to the figures provided by the VTC, from April 1995 to March 1996 the Insurance Training Centre supplied 70,000 trainee hours. The Technical College (Chai Wan) offers a three-year Higher Diploma in Insurance Studies, with 334 graduated in June 1996. Kwun Tong Technical Institute offers a full-time two-year Diploma in Insurance Studies, which has 67 students in 1996. Other certificate courses are also offered in addition.

Generally speaking, insurance practitioners are more interested in recognizable degrees and certificates rather than in general knowledge. Aside from courses offered by the local Insurance Institute of Hong Kong which gives a Diploma in Insurance Studies, training curriculum offered by The Chartered Insurance Institute (CII) and the Australian Insurance Institute (AII) have been quite popular in Hong Kong. Graduates of these programs will become associate members of the institute with titles of ACII and AAII respectively. Higher levels of course work will earn the title of Fellow, which is known as FCII or FAII, depending on whether it is the British or the Australian system, respectively. The Insurance Institute of New Zealand has also been offering courses.

In the area of life insurance, passing the examinations provided by Life Office Management Associations, LOMA, will earn one a title of Fellow of Life Management Institute, FLMI. The education and training of insurance practitioners in Hong Kong has also been enhanced through the U.S. Life Insurance Agency Management Association (LIMRA), often with the local co-operation of agent associations such as the HongKong Life Underwriter Association (LUA) and the newly formed General Agents and Management Association (GAMA). More channels and training possibilities are now being provided to agents in Hong Kong via the Life Underwriter Training Council (LUTC) and the Chartered Life Underwriter (CLU). The American College, with the assistance of the LUA and VTC, has also been able to provide courses for the CLU. The Extension Course Curriculum of the Baptist University also have courses that can be credited with the American College.

Judging from the large variety of courses and programmes available, insurance training in Hong Kong cannot be considered inadequate. The general impression is that there are a lot of job opportunities in the industry. It is possible, however, that even though there are job opportunities and training possibilities, people do not go into this line of trade. From the students' point of view, insurance is not a glamorous profession like investment banking, fund management, and regular banking business. This is an image issue arising from a lack of understand of what the insurance profession is about. Therefore, general business education in terms of explaining the role of insurance and how it functions will help improve the image of the industry.

Another avenue through which the profession can improve its image is by practitioners demonstrating their knowledge and their willingness to help clients solve problems in their business relationships. Vocational training, by implication, cannot supply the general knowledge attributable to a university degree. In-house training is also deficient in this respect, in that employees might know the products of their own companies very well but may have no knowledge of the products offered by their competitors. While industry-sponsored seminars can from time to time keep practitioners abreast of the latest development in the industry and the economy, these educational activities are voluntary and are not formally acknowledged in terms of certificates of recognition. In the long run, there will be an increasing demand for insurance practitioners to acquire general knowledge. Looking at the issue from this perspective, there is a question of whether or not training in the insurance industry of Hong Kong is adequate.

Last but not least, it is important to point out the linkage between insurance training and research. At the present moment, there is no such a linkage. Practitioners are prepared to take ready-made products and knowledge and apply them to the local setting. In view of the changing socio-economic environment in the area (as pointed out the previous chapter), however, there are many locally specific issues that text-book knowledge may be insufficient to answer. A case can be made to argue for a promotion of such a linkage. Research generates curiosity and interests. It is only when questions are raised that answers will be seek. Through this process, insurance curriculum in Hong Kong can be tailored-made with some "local flavor" — and thus increase the value-added of education for the profession.

Transparency

The question of transparency is intimately related to the organizational structure of a company, that is, how it is run. In Hong

Kong, only one insurance company is organized in the form of a stock company. While insurance contracts involving profit sharing are popular in Hong Kong, companies are not organized in the form of mutuals, as they are in the U.S. or in Europe. The insurance stock company in Hong Kong is called National Mutual, but it is not legally the same as a mutual. The lack of the latter kind of organization in Hong Kong may have more to do with tax reasons than with the underlying need to form mutuals in the region.In the U.S., a mutual company is organized under the state insurance code as a nonprofit corporation owned by the policyholders. This means that any excess income is either returned to the policyholders-owners as dividends, which is used to reduce premiums, or is retained to finance the future growth of the company. The insurance code in each state in the U.S. can vary in regard to its treatment of mutuals.[8]

A case can be made that mutuals are what the consumer in Hong Kong really wants. Consumers of life insurance products in Hong Kong usually prefer some forms of profit sharing with insurance companies. Out of a total of 2,178,629 non-linked life policies in force in Hong Kong in 1993, 1,437,699 (66%) opted for profit sharing, while an additional 64,529 policies opted for linked long-term products, which can also be considered some form of profit sharing (see Table 3.7 in Chapter 3). Regarding whole life policies, 95.5% of those in existence have variable pay-offs. This heavy reliance on the investment performance of insurance companies may indicate a need for more transparent insurance company operations.

The significance of the way in which ownership and institutional structure of an insurance company can affect its performance has not been much discussed in Hong Kong. In spite of the frequent discussions of this issue among academicians in the U.S.,[9] its implications cannot be easily examined in the Hong Kong setting. At present, Hong Kong is more sensitive to issues concerning consumer protection than to anything else. On this subject, Hong Kong is far behind other advanced areas in the world, where information can be more easily gathered. The equivalent of

U.S. insurance publications and watchdogs such as *National Underwriter Profiles*, *Life Insurance Fact Book*, *Best's Review*, *Best's Aggregates and Averages*, etc. are not found in Hong Kong. Likewise, supervision of the Consumer Council has been sporadic and on a case-by-case basis. Whether this trend is expected to continue or to gradually evolve into some regular type of governance structure is hard to determine. In view of the divergent life insurance products offered in the area, and of the possible difference between those offered here and elsewhere, a case can be made for the provision of more uniform comparisons of life insurance products to lower consumers' information costs.[10] The Hong Kong government has encouraged self regulation and self disclosure in this area. It is not clear, however, whether the Life Insurance Council of Hong Kong will take an active part in seeing that more uniform comparisons are actually made available.

The experience of how insurance industries elsewhere have organized to improve their transparency and therefore their credibility can be instructive for Hong Kong. For example, in 1970 in the U.S., a committee composed of representatives from eleven insurance companies was formed under the authority of three major life insurance company service organizations (American Life Convention, Institute of Life Insurance, and Life Insurance Association of America) to "consider the method or methods that a prospective buyer of life insurance may find most suitable for use in comparing the premiums, dividends and cash values of comparable policies that are offered by different life insurance companies". The result was a publication known as the *Report of the Joint Special Committee on Life Insurance Costs*.

The question of transparency is also closely related to the training issue mentioned previously. Agents' knowledge of their own and their competitors' products will give prospective clients additional confidence in the products they are buying. It is expected that insurance agents will need to become more generally knowledgeable as more and more investment-linked products are to be sold in the region.

Publicity Campaign

The public's perception of life insurance companies is quite subjective. It can range from complete mistrust of such organizations to complete reliance on them not only for security protection, but also for banking, investments, and general counseling. Life insurance agents sometimes perform an almost "missionary" role of putting one's life into perspective. Aside from giving policyholders the impression that the company the agent is representing is a good guardian of savings, some agents are successful because they can prompt a prospective customer to develop a benevolent bequest motive. In so doing, a great deal of trust must exist between the customer and the agent. In some situations, the insurance agent actually becomes the personal advisor for a customer's saving and consumption decisions.

There are, however, certain limits to what insurance agents can do. Ultimately, they are selling the insurance company's reputation. However, unlike other consumer products or even financial products such as banking and financial market investments, an insurance company's level of service cannot be evaluated until its customers make their claims. Between the time that a customer buys a contract and the time that he actually uses the service he has bought, there is a long period of inactivity during which he may need repeated assurance of the reliability of the product. Insurance companies' publicity campaigns, which can instill an image of them being as always ready to assist, are particularly important to the industry.

Insurance companies recognize the value of education, not only to employees working for the companies, but also to the general public about their companies and their products. Publicity campaigns in the form of scholarships, research funds, and the sponsoring of seminars, are some important ways in which insurance companies have already begun contributing to society. In order to effect changes in public perception, more and more innovative campaign programmes may have to be adopted.

Summary

Public perception of insurance companies and the need to upgrade their professional image have been discussed in this chapter. The demand for life insurance in Hong Kong has been evaluated in terms of penetration rates, willingness to pay, patterns of life insurance bought for others and reasons for not buying life insurance. Life insurance as a savings channel is further evaluated in terms of the public's perception of its use and its substitutability with other forms of savings. Public perception of insurance companies and agents is not overwhelmingly positive, but it is not as bad as individual complaint cases have made it out to be. Improvements in the public image of the profession have been discussed in terms of training and education, organizational changes of insurance companies towards increased transparency, and publicity campaigns demonstrating the industry's social consciousness.

Notes

1. Dionne and Eeckhoudt (1984) showed that under some risk-aversive assumptions, bank deposits and insurance are pure substitutes. Fischer (1973) and Richard (1975) modeled life insurance and saving. Borch (1990), p.241, derives an expression (equation 12) that shows that saving through life insurance takes place at a higher rate of interest than does conventional saving.

2. Huebner (1964) suggests that life insurance should provide a death payment equal to the insured future earnings. In spite of the endorsement of this idea from insurance texts and the American College of Life Underwriters, this does not appear to be the dominant marketing philosophy of any insurance company. See Borch (1990), p. 244.

3. The survey was not able to collect sufficient information for an estimation of the demand for life insurance in the sense that economists have used the term. Furthermore, financial questions have to be kept to a minimum to solicit a high response rate.

4. On the other hand, the response to a later question dealing with the respondents' impression of insurance agents, 56 of the 265 who had not bought life insurance (21.1%) said they have not been contacted by agents before. It is possible that the context in which the respondents answered this question is different from that in which they answered the subsequent

question. Either way, 21.1% does not appear to be a high number, either. This is to say that a great proportion of potential life insurance customers have already had some degree of exposure to agents attempting to sell life insurance.

5. For those respondents who had not bought life insurance for themselves but had bought insurance for others (nineteen usable observations only), seven had bought it for their spouses, six had bought it for their children, five had bought it for their parents, and one had bought it for another family of their.
6. *1993 Manpower Survey Report*, p.1.
7. *HK Economic Times*, 2 May 1996.
8. Green, Trieschmann, and Gustavson, p. 511.
9. Aside from the series of articles by Mayers and Smith, see also Hetherington (1969), Kreider (1972), and Anderson (1973).
10. In the U.S., there are standard insurance text that teach students how to make comparisons between different products. See for example the chapter on "Cost Analysis of Life Insurance and Annuities" in *Life Insurance*, by Kenneth Black, Jr. & Harold Skipper, Jr., 11th Ed., Prentice Hall: New Jersey, 1987.

CHAPTER 7

Conclusion and Policy Recommendations

Insurance, and life insurance in particular, is one of Hong Kong's fastest-growing industries. In 1994 gross insurance premiums in Hong Kong amounted to HK$39.2 billion, the fifth-highest figure in Asia. General and life insurance business contributed almost equally to this amount. With a technical reserve ratio of 99%, an overall net claims incurred ratio of 52.5% in general business, a penetration ratio of 40%, and an overall voluntary termination rate of a little over 10% in life insurance, the insurance industry in Hong Kong is alive and well, at least by several standard measures.

The three largest types of general insurance business in Hong Kong are motor vehicle insurance, property damage insurance, and general liability insurance, each of which occupies a significant percentage of the market. Motor vehicle and employee compensation insurance (included as general liability) are heavily competitive, with both exhibiting negative underwriting margins in 1992. While the motor vehicle insurance underwriting margin improved for two consecutive years following 1992, the general liability underwriting margin was still negative, at 4.2% in 1994. In the area of life insurance, whole life has the largest market share, while term insurance is not as popular in Hong Kong as it is in other countries in the West. For whole life insurance, profit participating policies outnumber nonprofit participating ones substantially.

The industry as a whole is an important non-bank sector of the financial sector of the economy. Although total premium represents only 3.8% of the GDP, the percentage of value added contributed by this sector, relative to the value added contributed by the other financial sectors, was between 8% and 12% from 1983 to 1993. Many of the insurance companies in Hong Kong are affiliated with banks. There is also a natural inclination for insurance companies to seek strategic alliances with other sectors of the economy such as real estate, shipping, and health care. Policies currently evaluated have focused on the industry itself, but a long-term view would have to recognize the interdependent nature of the business.

The insurance industry of Hong Kong has established its prominence in the insurance markets of Asia, but it is expected to go through evolutionary changes in the years to come. These changes will involve an interactive dynamics between the regulator, the insurance companies, the middlemen (agents and brokers), self-regulating bodies, and the consuming and the investing public.

Economic theories have been emphasized in this book as an *explanation* of some fundamental features of insurance contracts and the industrial organization of the industry, as a *suggestion* for formulating the relevant parameters for institutional development, and as a *proposal* for possible future areas of research. Specific issues of concern to the industry have been commented upon in the book. By broadly dividing them into three categories — one dealing with regulations, one dealing with competitive advantages, and one dealing with public image — we can summarize several basic trends in the future direction of the industry.

Three Basic Trends and Policy Discussion

First, as the line separating banks and non-banks in Hong Kong becomes blurred (and there are reasons to believe this is the case for the rest of the world), implications to the Hong Kong situation can be explored. While insurance companies can clearly operate independently, there are policy issues that may affect the insurance and banking sectors in an interrelated manner. There are macro issues such as savings and investment which are channeled through the insurance as well as the banking sector. But more importantly, the financial stability of the economic system as a whole via a "real estate-banking-insurance companies" linkage should be high on the agenda of the future government's policy consideration. To be sure, policy consideration in this area should only be precautionary in nature. There are private gains to be made from strategic alliance that would not require any policy assistance from the government. However, to the extent that private gains may entail social costs, and that the social costs in this case may only surface during a financial crisis of an economy, contingency plans should be made, and this planning task is quite within the realm of a responsible government.

Second, the insurance industry of Hong Kong is expected to be vastly affected by the China factor, the Mandatory Provident Fund (MPF) factor, and whatever industry policies the government develops in the years to come. The future policies would include reinsurance, captives, education and training, and the establishment and maintenance of guaranty funds. In deciding on a set of proactive policies of this type, one should bear in mind the paradigm of debate mentioned in the Introduction of this book: Are there sufficient reasons to believe that insurance supervision in Hong Kong should be elevated to a tool for economic policy? The question obviously cannot be answered easily, especially if Hong Kong is mandated to operate under a free enterprise system under the "One Country, Two Systems" framework. Any proactive policy would have to be consistent with a market competitive policy, which leaves the government with a very limited role, probably only as a facilitator of information and policy discussion. In the Introduction, we have discussed how an institutional structure can be evolved from an *atmosphere*. As Mr. Andrew Sheng of the Hong Kong Monetary Authority recently stated, "financial integration [of Hong Kong] with China is a trend, it cannot be a strategy." Indeed, unless there are compelling reasons, that may be the position that the future Insurance Authority wishes to take. However, to the extent that the government can more effectively co-ordinate the discussion of various policy implications, and to the extent that there is some hope that such implications can be efficiently implemented in the future, the government should continue to assist the industry in this attempt to conduct a constructive dialogue.

Third, policy makers may want to be aware that the future organization of the industry will be determined by a mix of driving forces coming from distribution, investment philosophies, and technology. Distribution has constituted an important aspect of the industry in Hong Kong in the past, but it may or may not be Hong Kong's competitive niche in terms of a broader development plan for the area in the years to come. The possibilities of cultivating a competitive niches for an investment emphasis (especially in light of the MPF factor) and the adoption and utilization of technology may also be considered. Whatever organizational structure the industry will move towards, there will be a need to improve the transparency of its operations in order to gain additional confidence from the public.

Specific Research Agenda for the Industry

Several topics deserve immediate attention:

Criteria for the Regulation of Commission Rates

Commission rates have so far been dealt with in an ad hoc manner, particularly in the areas of motor vehicle and employee compensation insurance. In the last couple of years, government policy on this issue has appeared to flip-flop without achieving uniform consensus. Theoretically, rate regulation is likely to result in a reduction in service quality, which could in turn result in an overall reduction in economic efficiency; however, there are claims that commission rates have been "excessive". Whether rates are to be government imposed or self regulated, the industry needs to develop more coherent policy guidelines on this issue.

Criteria for a Reorganization of Intermediaries

Since 1993 government has been wanting to draw a clearer distinction between brokers and agents. The Insurance Authority has so far taken a flexible stand, letting the industry self regulate, but perhaps the underlying reason for reorganization needs to be re-examined. On economic theory alone, the reason for a strong demarcation is weak, and in practice, the market environment may call for a different organization mode. The suggestion here, therefore is to conduct an in-depth study of the 2134 establishments listed by the Census and Statistics Department for insurance agents, brokers, and other insurance services. This is for the purpose of understanding the current situation and to evaluate what, if any, action should be taken to reorganize the middlemen market of the insurance industry.

Effects of Local Asset Maintenance

The local asset maintenance ordinance introduced in 1995 requires a general insurer to keep 80% of its liability in local assets. Theoretically, directly regulating the form of investment cannot assist the industry in terms of its investment performance. While the additional constraints imposed might not be binding in the sense that the banks' issue of unconditional and irrevocable letters of credit may provide sufficient amount to meet the 80% constraint, there are likely to be additional costs on the portfolio management of insurance assets. The empirical questions are how much stability the 80% constraints will be able to bring, how much of the bank involvement has been relied upon, and what may be the spillover effects on the banking industry.

The Effects of the MPF Factor

The proposed Mandatory Provident Fund that the Hong Kong Government has been considering will generate a sizable pool of savings (about HK$20 to HK$40 billion a year) that retirement funds and insurance companies can access. Insurance companies in Hong Kong may be able to more effectively utilize their experience and marketing skills in their competition with the retirement funds, because the philosophical foundation behind the MPF is merely enforced savings. To do so, however, the insurance industry needs to establish itself as an important area of investment and a savings channel in the economy. So far, the industry has not made a concerted effort in this direction.

Training and Education

Currently, the competitive supply of professional certificates in the industry are of the "garden variety". There will be some need to simplify and unify the curriculum. In terms of the profession's real demands, the emergence of new products such as the linked products, the large marketing effort required for the MPF, and the opening of the China market all point to a need for more knowledgeable and professional insurance practitioners in the industry. In addition, if a proactive policy stand on the insurance industry is to be pursued, a broader knowledge base for the training of personnel will be required.

Reinsurance and Captives Potential

At the time of this writing (1997), specific proposals on reinsurance and captives by the government's ad hoc committee has not yet been announced. But the issue cannot be tackled purely from the point of view of tax relief. What is more important is to articulate a governance structure that would involve big players in the field of insurance as well as the government in China, and possibly Taiwan also, in order to create a viable strategy. While some comments have been made here, developing the potential of reinsurance and captives is expected to be an on-going process. The pursuit of such initiatives by the Hong Kong Government can be an indication that insurance policy is going to be elevated to the level as a tool of economic policy. This will not necessarily be a bad idea if the new strategy can be kept consistent with a free market competition policy.

Appendix A

The World's 50 Largest Insurers ranked by assets as determined by Worldscope; figures are based on each company's 1994 fiscal-year results (in millions of U.S. dollars on 31 December 1994); exchange rates and percentage changes are based on home currencies.

Source: Asian Wall Street Journal, Oct. 23, 1995.

Rank					
1994	1993	Company (Country)	Assets	Capital	Net Income
1	1	Nippon Life (Japan)	$348,579	$4,164	$3,042
2	3	Zenkyoren (Japan)	247,700	3,554	319
3	4	Dai-Ichi Mutual Life (Japan)	245,926	3,412	2,184
4	5	Sumitomo Life (Japan)	214,835	3,067	2,202
5	2	Prudential Insurance (U.S.)	211,902	11,711	−1,175
6	8	Allianz Holding (Germany)	164,601	13,759	620
7	7	Compagnie UAP (France)	160,376	17,369	294
8	10	Meiji Mutual Life (Japan)	148,640	2,498	1,582
9	6	Axa (France)	145,031	13,470	425
10	9	Metropolitan Life (U.S.)	131,177	8,285	106
11	11	American International Group (U.S.)	114,346	27,047	2,176
12	15	Asahi Mutual Life (Japan)	112,139	1,501	965
13	14	Prudential (U.K.)	98,063	13,041	635
14	12	Equitable (U.S.)	94,640	5,818	324
15	13	Aetna Life & Casualty (U.S.)	92,906	6,790	468
16	17	Mitsui Mutual Life (Japan)	92,779	1,112	872
17	16	Cigna (U.S.)	83,838	7,200	554
18	24	Internationale Nederlanden Groep (Netherlands)	82,163	12,092	799
19	21	Yasuda Mutual Life (Japan)	82,050	1,742	1,203

Rank					
1994	1993	Company (Country)	Assets	Capital	Net Income
20	23	Assurances Generals de France (France)	79,681	16,735	165
21	22	Aegon (Netherlands)	78,992	8,865	663
22	18	State Farm (U.S.)	76,667	21,165	–229
23	19	Teachers Insurance & Annuity (U.S.)	73,348	5,103	N.A.
24	25	Tokio Marine & Fire (Japan)	72,990	22,320	1,989
25	38	Commercial Union (U.K.)	72,715	9,235	4546
26	27	Zurich Insurance (Switzerland)	69,931	8,871	532
27	20	New York Life (U.S.)	68,926	4,958	404
28	30	Assicurazioni Generali (Italy)	64,066	8,580	397
29	28	Allstate (U.S.)	61,369	9,295	484
30	26	Travelers (U.S.)	61,136	N.A.	839
31	29	Standard Life Assurance (U.K.)	58,512	8,434	N.A.
32	45	Winterthur Group (Switzerland)	56,179	4,579	278
33	31	Australian Mutual (Australia)	51,882	6,566	N.A.
34	40	Swiss Life Insurance & Pension (Switzerland)	50,636	2,585	998
35	32	Norwich Union (U.K.)	50,100	5,721	N.A.
36	34	John Hancock Mutual Life (U.S.)	49,805	3,183	183
37	43	Swiss Reinsurance (Switzerland)	49,603	5,439	248
38	33	Lincoln National (U.S.)	49,028	3,462	350
39	36	Northwestern Mutual (U.S.)	48,112	3,415	398
40	35	Legal & General (U.K.)	47,891	5,854	174
41	39	Nationwide (U.S.)	47,696	4,820	445
42	37	American General (U.S.)	46,295	8,653	513
43	42	Yasuda Fire & Marine (Japan)	45,430	9,912	N.A.
44	46	Fortis (Belgium/Netherlands)	45,346	6,153	N.A.
45	47	Aachener und Muenchener (Germany)	44,885	2,302	135
46	44	Principal Mutual Life (U.S.)	44,117	2,719	152
47	–	Sun Life Assurance (Canada)	42,979	3,481	N.A.
48	–	Daido Mutual Life (Japan)	42,901	691	458
49	50	Societe Central du Gan (France)	42,735	3,055	–735
50	41	CNA Financial (U.S.)	42,658	5,556	37

Appendix B

Table B.1
GDP, Gross Premium, and Penetration Ratio

Year	GDP HK$ million	Gross Premium HK$ million	Penetration Ratio HK$ million
1982	192,488	4,771	2.48
1983	212,673	6,254	2.94
1984	256,493	7,535	2.94
1985	271,655	8,760	3.22
1986	312,561	10,658	3.41
1987	384,488	12,145	3.16
1988	455,022	13,585	2.99
1989	523,861	15,819	3.02
1990	582,549	18,975	3.26
1991	668,512	23,083	3.45
1992	779,335	28,021	3.60
1993	897,595	33,986	3.79

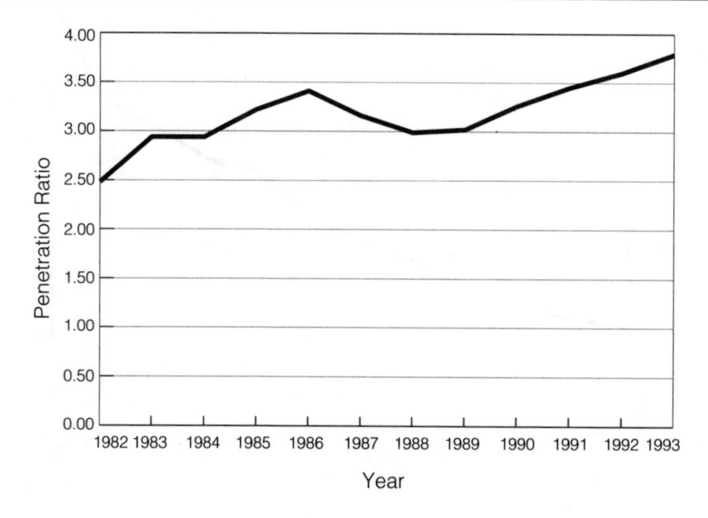

Source: Census & Statistics Department, Hong Kong, *Estimates of Gross Domestic Product 1961–1994*, March 1995.
Census & Statistics Department, Hong Kong, *Survey of Storage, Communication, Financing, Insurance & Business Services,* 1982–1993.

Table B.2
Employment Size

Year	Number of Employees
1982	5,546
1983	5,993
1984	6,739
1985	7,334
1986	9,168
1987	10,136
1988	11,666
1989	14,244
1990	14,852
1991	16,630
1992	18,114
1993	23,917

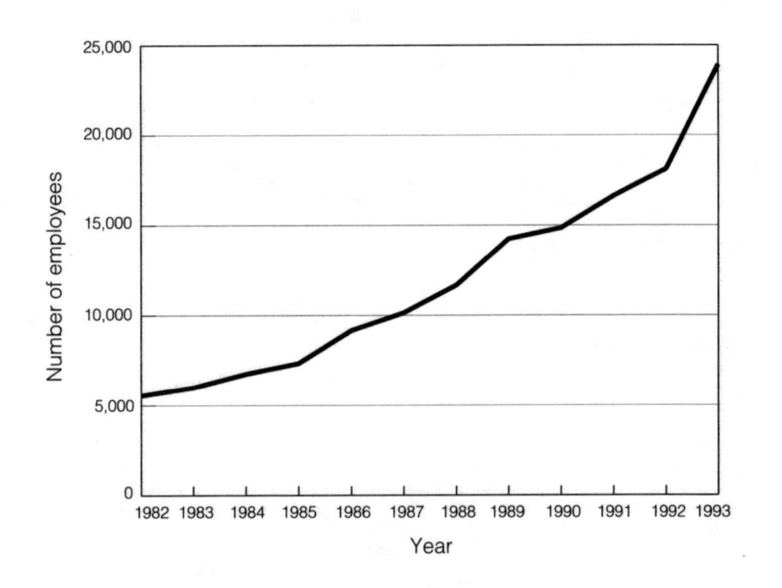

Source: Census & Statistics Department, Hong Kong, *Survey of Storage, Communication, Financing, Insurance & Business Services*, 1982–1993.

Table B.3
Density (Per-head Direct Gross Premium)

Year	Population (million)	Gross Premium in Direct Business (HK$ million)	Density (HK$)
1982	5.26	2988.639	567.69
1983	5.35	3925.954	734.49
1984	5.40	4777.193	885.01
1985	5.46	5240.299	960.42
1986	5.51	7208.589	1309.42
1987	5.58	8147.444	1459.97
1988	5.63	9814.091	1743.91
1989	5.69	12,204.722	2144.94
1990	5.70	15179.666	2661.00
1991	5.75	18931.915	3289.76
1992	5.81	22780.369	3919.87
1993	5.92	27577.305	4659.10

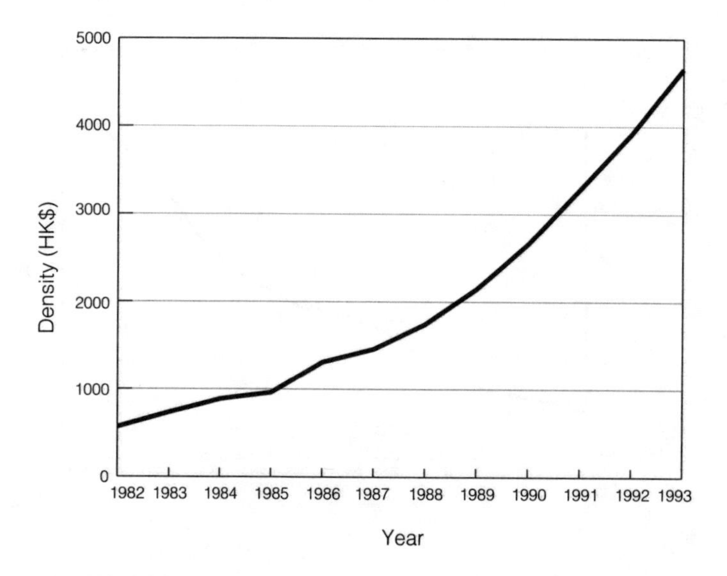

Source: Census & Statistics Department, Hong Kong, *Estimates of Gross Domestic Product 1961–1994*, March 1995.
Census & Statistics Department, Hong Kong, *Survey of Storage, Communication, Financing, Insurance & Business Services*, 1982–1993.

Table B.4
Funds and Reserves

Year	Funds and Reserves (HK$ thousand)
1982	5,419,480
1983	7,139,672
1984	7,986,282
1985	10,454,420
1986	14,713,396
1987	17,446,260
1988	18,565,838
1989	21,661,430
1990	26,149,598
1991	34,486,679
1992	39,699,894
1993	41,184,346

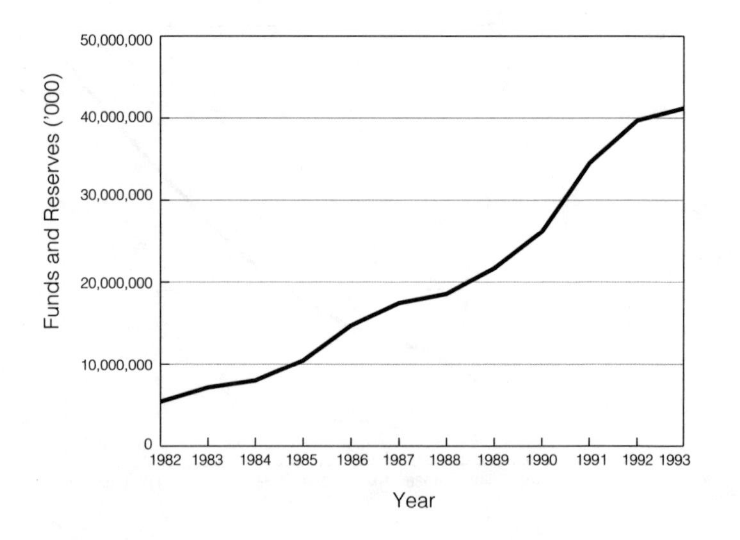

Source: Census & Statistics Department, Hong Kong, *Survey of Storage, Communication, Financing, Insurance & Business Services,* 1982–1993.

Table B.5
Claims and Expenses

Year	Claims and Expenses (HK$ thousand)
1982	1,952,299
1983	2,561,532
1984	2,939,719
1985	3,627,326
1986	4,098,798
1987	5,515,487
1988	7,999,819
1989	8,958,257
1990	10,157,713
1991	12,656,700
1992	16,558,815
1993	18,316,506

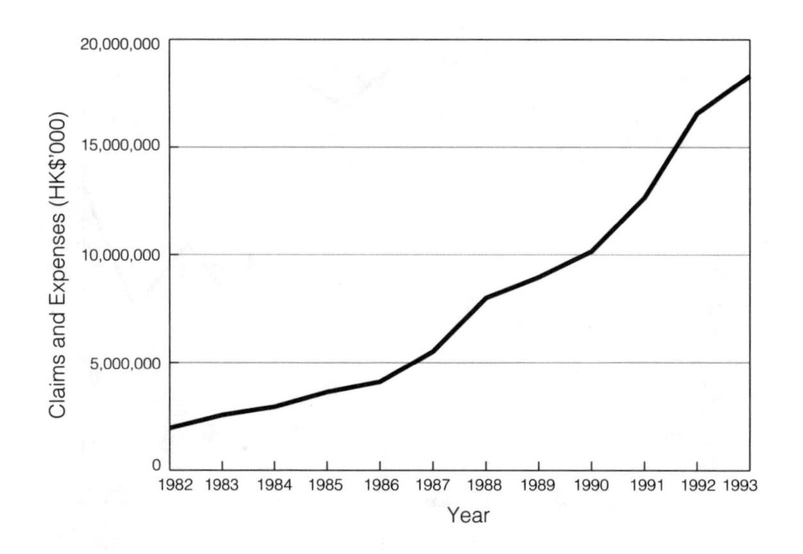

Source: Census & Statistics Department, Hong Kong, *Survey of Storage, Communication, Financing, Insurance & Business Services,* 1982–1993.

Note: Claims and expenses = Net claims + Operating expenses + Compensation of employees.

Table B.6
Number of Establishment
(General and Life Insurers)

Year	Number of Establishments
1982	181
1983	173
1984	176
1985	184
1986	183
1987	183
1988	179
1989	182
1990	161
1991	167
1992	161
1993	172

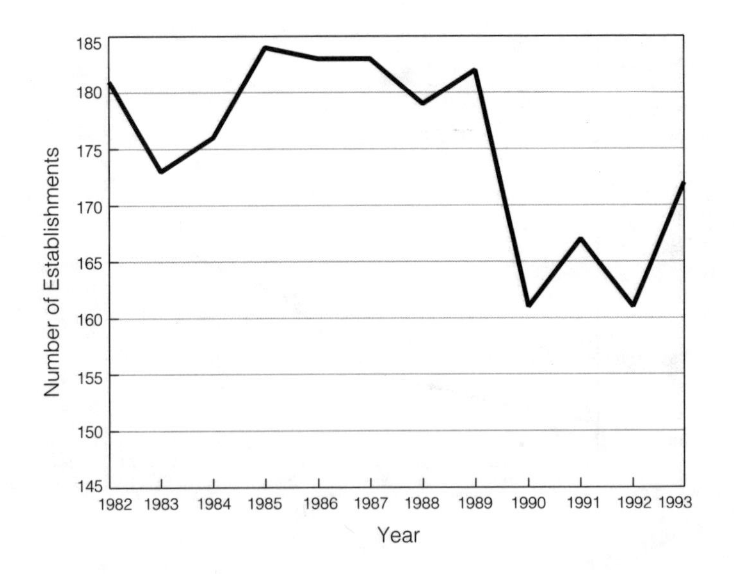

Source: Census & Statistics Department, Hong Kong, *Survey of Storage, Communication, Financing, Insurance & Business Services*, 1982–1993.

Appendix C

Insurance Companies Ordinance, Chapter 4
Eighth Schedule

Assets which qualify as assets in Hong Kong.

1. The following qualify as assets in Hong Kong:
   (a) real property, including a leasehold interest therein, located in Hong Kong;
   (b) computer equipment, office machinery, furniture, motor vehicles and other equipment located in Hong Kong;
   (c) money, in any currency or monetary unit, deposited at an authorized institutions as defined in the Banking Ordinance (Cap. 155);
   (d) bonds or other securities issued in Hong Kong provided that they are transferable and registrable at a register in Hong Kong and, in the case of bonds or other securities which are evidenced by certificates, the certificates for them are for the time being kept in Hong Kong;
   (e) bonds or other securities issued outside Hong Kong, the certificates for which are for the time being kept in Hong Kong and which are transferable by delivery, with or without endorsement;
   (f) negotiable bills of exchange, within the meaning of the Bills of Exchange Ordinance (Cap. 19), or other negotiable instruments which are for the time being kept in Hong Kong;
   (g) shares in respect of a company, wherever incorporated and whether or not it comes within the definition of "company" in section 2(1) of this Ordinance, which shares are:
      (i) transferable and registrable only at a register in Hong Kong; or
      (ii) in the ordinary course of business, transferred and

registered at a register in Hong Kong and the certificates for which (if any) are for the time being kept in Hong Kong;

(h) debts that may be enforced only by legal proceedings in a Hong Kong court, other than amounts recoverable in respect of claims outstanding under reinsurance contracts ceded;

(i) an interest in a "unit trust", as defined in the Securities Ordinance (Cap. 333), which is realizable in Hong Kong and in respect of which the governing law of the trust is expressly stated to be that of Hong Kong to the exclusion of all others.

Bibliography

1. Akerlof, G. A. (1970). "The Market for 'Lemons': Quality Uncertainty and the Market Mechanism," *Quarterly Journal of Economics*, 84.
2. Allais, M. (1953). "Generalisation des theories de l'equilibre economique general et du rendement social aucas du risque," *Econometrie*, Paris:CNRS.
3. American Council of Life Insurance (1994). *Life Insurance Fact Book.*
4. Anderson, Buist M. (1973). "Policyholder Control of a Mutual Life Insurance Company," 22 Cleveland ST. L. Rev. 439.
5. Arrow, K. J.(1953). "Le Role des valeurs boursieres pour la repartition la meilleure des risques," *Econometrie*, Paris : CNRS.
6. _______ (1963). "Uncertainty and the Welfare Economics of Medical Care," *The American Economic Review*, 53.
7. _______ (1965). "Insurance, Risk and Resources Allocation," in Arrow, K. J. (1965), *Aspects of the Theory of Risk Bearing.* Helsinki: Yrjo Jahnsson Foundation.
8. _______ (1974). "Optimal Insurance and Generalized Deductibles," Scandinavian Actuarial Journal, 1.
9. Bawcutt, P.A. (1991). *Captive Insurance Companies.* New York: Woodhead-Faulkner.
10. Black, Kenneth, Jr. and Skipper, Harold, Jr. (1987). *Life Insurance*, 11th ed. Prentice Hall: New Jersey.
11. Borch, K. (1990). *Economics of Insurance.* Amsterdam : North Holland.
12. _______ (1962). "Equilibrium in a Reinsurance Market," Econometrica, 30.
13. _______. *(1960) The Safety Loading of Reinsurance Premiums. Skandinavisk Akttuarietidskrift.*
14. _______ (1961). *"The Utility Concept Applied to Theory of Insurance," Astin Bulletin*, 1.

15. Brown, A. (1973). *Hazard Unlimited. The Story of Lloyd's of London.* London: Peter Davies Ltd.

16. Buchanan, James M. (1990). "The Domain of Constitutional Economics," *Constitutional Political Economy*, 1.

17. Census and Statistics Department of the Hong Kong Government, *Survey of Storage, Communication, Financing, Insurance & Business Services*, 1982–1993.

18. _______ (1995). *Estimates of Gross Domestic Product 1961–1994*, March 1995.

19. Chernik, Vladimir P. (1970). *The Consumer's Guide to Insurance Buying*. U.S.: Sherbourne Press.

20. Cheung, Steven N. S. (1969). *The Theory of Share Tenancy. Chicago: The University of Chicago Press.*

21. Churchill, Lawrence (1996). "Future Prospects for Bancassurance and its Impact on the Global Insurance Industry," speech delivered at *Emerging Asian Insurance Markets Conference*, March 1996, Hong Kong.

22. Crocker, K. J. and Snow, A. (1985). "The efficiency of Competitive Equilibria in Insurance Markets with Adverse Selection," Journal of Public Economics, 26.

23. Cummins, J. David (1975). *An Econometric Model of the Life Insurance Sector of the U.S. Economy*. U.S.: Heath.

24. Cummins, J. David and Lamm-Tennant, Joan (1993). *Financial Management of Life Insurance Companies*. U.S.: KAP.

25. Denney, V. (1996). "US Brokers: times are changing," *Global Risk Management., The Winchester Group.*

26. Dionne, G. and Eeckhoudt, L. (1984). "Insurance and Saving : Some Further Results," Insurance : Mathematics and Economics, 3.

27. Dionne, G. and Harrington, S.E. (1990). *Foundations of Insurance Economics: Readings in Economics and Finance. Boston: Kluwer Academic Publisher.*

28. Dobbyn, John F. (1981). *Insurance Law in a Nutshell.* U.S.: West,

29. Ehrlich, J. and Becker, G. (1972). "Market Insurance, Self Insurance and Self Protection," *Journal of Political Economy*, 80.

30. Ennew, C., Watkins, T. and Wright, M. (1990). *Marketing Financial Services*, 2nd ed. Jordan Hill, Oxford: Heinemann Professional Pub.

31. Etgar, M. (1977). "Cost Effectiveness in Insurance Distribution," *Journal of Risk and Insurance*, 44.

32. Finsinger, G.. (1986). *The Economics of Insurance Regulation: A Cross-National Study., Berlin: WZB-Publication.*

33. Fisher S. (1973). "A Life Cycle Model of Life Insurance Purchasing," *International Economic Review*, 14.

34. Flanigan, G., Winkler, D., and Johnson, J. (1993)., "Cost Differences of Distribution Systems by Line in the Property and Liability Insurance Industry," *Journal of Insurance Issues*, 16.

35. Friedman, M. and L. J. Savage (1948). "The Utility Analysis of Choices Involving Risk," *Journal of Political Economy*, 56.

36. Gaines, P., Jr., ed. (1970). *Cost Facts on Life Insurance: The Interest-Adjusted Method.* The National Underwriting Company.

37. Greene, Trieschmann and Gustavson (1992). *Risk & Insurance.* Cincinnati Ohio*:* South-Western, 8th Edition.

38. Hansmann, H. (1985). "The Organization of Insurance Companies: Mutual versus Stock," *Journal of Law, Economics, and Organization*, 1.

39. Hetherington, J. A. C. (1969), "Fact v. Fiction : Who Owns Mutual Insurance Companies," 4 Wisc. Law Rev. 1068.

40. Hiebert, L. D. (1989). "Optimal Loss Reduction and Risk Aversion," *Journal of Risk and Insurance*, 56.

41. Ho, Ben (1995). "Emerging Insurance Markets in Far East," *The Geneva Papers on Risk and Insurance*, 20.

42. Hongkong and Shanghai Banking Corporation Limited (1995). *The Insurance Industry in Hong Kong 1995.*

43. Hong Kong Insurance Claims Complaint Board (1994). *Annual Report 1994.*

44. Hong Kong Insurance Training Board, Vocation Training Council (1993). *1993 Manpower Survey Report: Insurance Industry.*

45. Hubbard, R. Glenn (1994). *Money, the Financial System and the Economy,. Mass.: Addison-Wesley Publishing Co.*

46. Huebner, S. S. (1964). "Human Life Values — Role of Life Insurance," *Life Insurance Handbook*, 2nd edition. Richard D. Irwin, Homewood, III.

47. The Insurance Institute of Hong Kong (1981). *IIHK Journal*, July 1981.

48. Jonathan, E. (1995). "Market Report: Bermuda," *The Review: Worldwide Reinsurance*, September 1995.

49. Joskow, P. J. (1973). "Cartels, Competition and Regulation in the

Property-Liability Insurance Industry," *Bell Journal of Economics and Management Science,* 4.

50. Kihlstrom R. E. and Pauly, M. (1971) "The Role of Insurance in the Allocation of Risk," American Economic Review, 49.

51. Kihlstrom, R. E. and Roth, A. E. (1982). "Risk Aversion and the Negotiation of Insurance Contracts," Journal of Risk and Insurance, 49.

52. Klein, B., Crawfor, R. G. and Alchian, A. A. (1978). "Vertical Integration, Appropriable Rents, and the Competitive Contracting Process," *Journal of Law and Economics*, 21.

53. Kreider, Gary (1972). "Who Owns the Mutuals? Proposals for Reform of Membership Rights in Mutual Insurance and Banking Companies," 41 Cincinnati L. Rev. 275.

54. Kwong, Louis S. K. (1987). *A Study of the Profits of Local General Insurance Companies*. MBA thesis, The University of Hong Kong.

55. Lau, Steven (1996). "Hong Kong into the 21st Century: The Servicing Economy," speech delivered at the *Symposium on Service Promotion*, 12 March 1996. Hong Kong.

56. Lee, C. G., Hamwi, I. S. and Niroomand F. (1995). "Scale and Scope Economies for Direct Writers in the Property-Liability Insurance Industry," *The Journal of Insurance Issues,* 19.

57. Louberge, Henri (1990). *Risk, Information and Insurance. U.S.: KAP.*

58. Lyon, E. A., ed. (1993). *National Underwriter Profiles, Life Insurers Edition.*

59. Marvel, Howard P. (1982). "Exclusive Dealing," Journal of Law & Economics, vol. XXV, April 1982.

60. Mayers, D. and Smith, C.W. (1981). "Contractual Provisions, Organizational Structure, and Conflict Control in Insurance Markets," Journal of Business, 54.

61. _______ (1982). "On the Corporate Demand for Insurance," *Journal of Business*, 55.

62. _______ (1986). "Ownership Structure and Control: The Mutualization of Stock Life Insurance Companies," Journal of Financial Economics, 16.

63. _______ (1988). "Ownership Structure Across Lines of Property — Casualty Insurance," *The Journal of Law and Economics,* 31.

64. Mishkin, Ferderic S. (1995). *Financial Markets, Institutions, and Money.* New York: Harpercollins College Publishers.

65. Moffet, D. (1977). "Optimal Deductible and Consumption Theory," Journal of Risk and Insurance, 44.

66. _______ (1975). "*Risk Bearing and Consumption Theory,*" *Astin Bulletin*, 18.

67. OECD, *Insurance Statistics Yearbook 1986-1993*. 1995 Edition.

68. Office of Commissioner of Insurance And the Registrar of Occupational Retirement Schemes, Hong Kong, *Annual Report 1994*.

69. Pan, Lufu (1996). "Present and Future of China's Insurance Market," speech delivered at a seminar on April 24, 1996, Hong Kong.

70. Pauly, M. V. (1974). "Overinsurance and Public Provision of Insurance: The Role of Moral Hazard and Adverse Selection," Quarterly Journal of Economics, 88.

71. Piper, A. (1995). "Re/ Insurance Brokers Face a Challenging Future," *The Review: Worldwide Reinsurance*, October 1995.

72. Reddy, N. (1995). "How Much Do You Pay Your Broker," *The Review: Worldwide Reinsurance*, June 1995.

73. Richard S. F. (1975). "Optimal Consumption, Portfolio and Life Insurance : Rules for an Uncertain Lived Individual in a Continuous Time Model," Journal of Financial Economics, 187–203.

74. Ross, S. (1973). "The Economic Theory of Agency: The Principal's Problem," American Economic Review, 63.

75. Rothschild, M. and Stiglitz, J. E. (1960), "Equilibrium in Competitive Insurance Markets: The Economics of Markets with Imperfect Information," *Quarterly Journal of Economics*, 90.

76. Santomero, A. M. (1993). "Banking and Insurance: A Banking Industry Perspective," from *Financial Management of Life Insurance Companies* edited by Cummins, J. D. and Lamm-Tennant, J., Boston: Kluwer Academic Publishers.

77. _______ and Chung, E. C. (1992). "Evidence in Support of Broader Bank Powers," *Journal of Financial Markets, Institutions and Instruments*, 1.

78. Schlesinger, H. (1981). "The Optimal Level of Deductibility in Insurance Contracts," *Journal of Risk and Insurance*, 48.

79. SCOR TECH, *Bancassurance*, December 1993.

80. Spence, M. and Zeckhauser, R. (1971). "Insurance, Information and Individual Action," American Economic Review, 61.

81. Stiglitz, G. J. (1977). "Monopoly, Non-Linear Pricing and Imperfect Information : The Insurance Market," *Review of Economic Studies*, 44.

82. The Swiss Reinsurance Company: Zurich, *Insurance Markets of the World.* 1964.

83. Tashjian, P. C. and Cooray, A. (1995). *Regulatory Framework of Finance and Banking in Hong Kong.* Hong Kong: Longman.

84. Valerie Denney (1996), "US brokers: times are changing," *Global Risk Manager.* The Winchestor Group, Regent Publications Ltd.

85. Von Neumann, J. and Morgenstern, O. (1947). *Theory of Games and Economic Behavior.* Princeton: Princeton University Press.

86. Watson Wyatt Worldwide, *Annual Report 1995: Measurement of Investment Performance Survey for Hong Kong Retirement Schemes.*

87. _______. *A Guide to the China Insurance Market.* 1996.

88. The Winchester Group, *Global Reinsurance.* March 1996 – May 1996, Regent Publications Ltd.

89. Webb, B. L., Launie, J. J., Rokes, W. P. and Baglini, N. A. (1984). *Insurance Company Operation*, 3rd Edition. Pennsylvania, American Institute for Property and Liability Underwriters, Inc., 1984.

90. Williamson, O. E. (1985). *The Economic Institutions of Capitalism: Firms, Markets, Relational Contracting.* New York: Collier Macmillan.

91. Winter, R. A. (1990). "Moral Hazard in Insurance Contracts," in G. Dionne (ed.), *Contributions to Insurance Economics.* Boston: Kluwer Academic Publishers.

92. Wong, Jim H. Y. (1991). "Hong Kong's Insurance Industry," from *The Hong Kong Financial System*, ed. by Yan, Richard Ki Ho, Scott, Robert Haney and Wong, Kie Ann. Hong Kong: Oxford University Press.

93. Wood, J. (1995). "Virgin Territory," *International Risk Management*, July/August.

94. _______ (1995). "Captivated in Cayman," *International Risk Management*, July/August, 1995.

95. Yeung, Terry C. S. (1990). "A Strategic Study of the General Insurance Industry in Hong Kong," MBA thesis, The University of Hong Kong.

96. Yip, C. W. (1994). "An analysis of the Structure of Hong Kong Insurance Market and its Commercial Prospects for Foreign Insurance Companies," MA. thesis, School of Accounting, Banking and Economics, University of Wales.

Index

About the Author

A native of Hong Kong, Ben T. Yu received his PhD from the University of Washington. He is Professor of Economics with California State University at Northridge. Dr. Yu is also Associate Director of the Center for Insurance Education and Research in the United States. Now in Hong Kong, he serves as a consultant to the Education Committee of the Asian Venture Capital Institute. While teaching a course on Capital Theory at The University of Hong Kong, he actively develops a course bearing the same title on the Internet where, as of May 1997, the Web-site is http://www.econ.hku.hk/course/benyu/.

The Hong Kong Economic Policy Studies Series

Titles	*Authors*
Hong Kong and the Region	
❑ The Political Economy of Laissez Faire	Yue-Chim Richard WONG
❑ Hong Kong and South China: The Economic Synergy	Yun-Wing SUNG
❑ Inflation in Hong Kong	Alan K. F. SIU
❑ Trade and Investment: Mainland China, Hong Kong and Taiwan	K. C. FUNG
❑ Tourism and the Hong Kong Economy	Kai-Sun KWONG
❑ Economic Relations between Hong Kong and the Pacific Community	Yiu-Kwan FAN
Money and Finance	
❑ The Monetary System of Hong Kong	Y. F. LUK
❑ The Linked Exchange Rate System	Yum-Keung KWAN Francis T. LUI
❑ Hong Kong as an International Financial Centre: Evolution, Prospects and Policies	Y. C. JAO
❑ Corporate Governance: Listed Companies in Hong Kong	Richard Yan-Ki HO Stephen Y. L. CHEUNG
❑ Institutional Development of the Insurance Industry	Ben T. YU
Infrastructure and Industry	
❑ Technology and Industry	Kai-Sun KWONG
❑ Competition Policy and the Regulation of Business	Leonard K. CHENG Changqi WU
❑ Telecom Policy and the Rise of Digital Media	Milton L. MUELLER
❑ Port Facilities and Container Handling Services	Leonard K. CHENG Yue-Chim Richard WONG

Titles	*Authors*
❑ Efficient Transport Policy	Timothy D. HAU Stephen CHING
❑ Competition in Energy	Pun-Lee LAM
❑ Privatizing Water and Sewage Services	Pun-Lee LAM Yue-Cheong CHAN

Immigration and Human Resources

❑ Labour Market in a Dynamic Economy	Wing SUEN William CHAN
❑ Immigration and the Economy of Hong Kong	Kit Chun LAM Pak Wai LIU
❑ Youth, Society and the Economy	Rosanna WONG Paul CHAN

Housing and Land

❑ The Private Residential Market	Alan K. F. SIU
❑ On Privatizing Public Housing	Yue-Chim Richard WONG
❑ Housing Policy for the 21st Century: Homes for All	Rosanna WONG
❑ Financial and Property Markets: Interactions Between the Mainland and Hong Kong	Pui-King LAU
❑ Town Planning in Hong Kong: A Critical Review	Lawrence Wai-Chung LAI

Social Issues

❑ Retirement Protection: A Plan for Hong Kong	Francis T. LUI
❑ Income Inequality and Economic Development	Hon-Kwong LUI
❑ Health Care Reform: An Economic Perspective	Lok-Sang HO
❑ Economics of Crime and Punishment	Siu Fai LEUNG